Waltzes
I Have Not
Forgotten

Waltzes
I Have Not
Forgotten

Bernadette Gabay Dyer

WOMEN'S PRESS
TORONTO

Waltzes I Have Not Forgotten
Bernadette Gabay Dyer

First published in 2004 by
Women's Press, an imprint of Canadian Scholars' Press Inc.
180 Bloor Street West, Suite 801
Toronto, Ontario
M5S 2V6

www.womenspress.ca

Waltzes I Have Not Forgotten is a work of fiction set during the turbulent
times of the twentieth century. Although some background events are based
on historical fact, the characters and their encounters are fictitious,
and live only in the imagination of the author.

Canadian Scholars' Press/Women's Press gratefully acknowledges financial support for our publishing activities from the Ontario Arts Council, the Canada
Council for the Arts, the Government of Canada through the Book Publishing
Industry Development Program (BPIDP), and the Government of Ontario
through the Ontario Book Publishing Tax Credit Program.

National Library of Canada Cataloguing in Publication Data
Dyer, Bernadette Gabay
Waltzes I have not forgotten / by Bernadette Gabay Dyer.

ISBN 0-88961-443-1
I. Title.

PS8557.Y47W34 2004   C813'.54   C2003-905891-3

Cover art by Bernadette Gabay Dyer
Cover design by Drew Hawkins
Text design and layout by Linda Mackey
Author photo by R.G. Taylor

04   05   06   07   08   5   4   3   2   1

Printed and bound in Canada by AGMV Marquis Imprimeur, Inc.

For Teddy and Marguerite Gabay,
with Love & Gratitude.

May the rest of us share in their enjoyment.

Table of Contents

Acknowledgements

Special thanks are owed to the following individuals, who read this manuscript, and offered encouragement: Terry Sweeney, Terry Dyer, Delores Sloan, Cheryl Philips, Anne-Marie Smith, and Althea Prince and her colleagues at CSPI/Women's Press. Thanks also to Kathleen Griffin for her memories of Luke Lane.

Introduction

My mother, Margaret Moneague, was murdered in Jamaica in 1919. History will not speak of her or record how valiantly she, who was little more than a child, struggled to survive against overwhelming poverty. History will be preoccupied with the lack of unionization of Kingston's dock workers, the rise and fall of sugar cane prices, the precarious banana industry and its association with the United Fruit Company. And history will elaborate on the devastation caused by earthquakes and hurricanes earlier in the century. But it will not record the riveting circumstances of my birth, in the back streets of Kingston, or my subsequent life. Therefore it is I, John Moneague, who am compelled to speak of it.

Part One

CHAPTER 1

Kingston

My mother, a poor uneducated orphan, came from the rural parish of St. Mary on the northeast coast of Jamaica. She had intended to find work as a servant in the capital city of Kingston, and spent her last sixpence obtaining a ride on an oxen-drawn coconut cart heading for the city. The cartwheels rumbled noisily over rough terrain, past lush crops of coconuts and bananas, as wild goats ambled along a narrow path.

My mother's thin, dark-skinned legs dangled and swayed over the back of the cart as she rested snugly against musty jute sacks of water coconuts, holding on tightly to a small frayed thread bag, which she had filled with a few mangoes, sticks of sugarcane, and three oranges, thinking that would tide her over until she found work.

On arriving in Kingston, she was intrigued by the clangour, the confusion, and the crowds. She craned her neck, staring astonished at the buggies, bicycles, carts, and tramcars as the cart laboriously made its way past colonial-style churches, imposing government buildings, clothing stores, grocery shops, and houses.

She was unprepared when the coconut vendor finally stopped the cart. "This is far as I go," he said, pulling the cart over beside an ornate metal fence running alongside a large, well-kept public garden in the heart of the downtown area. "Dis is Parade Gardens," he said absently, waving his veined hand in the air. "And that over dey is Victoria Park," he continued, no doubt noticing the bewildered expression on my mother's face. "It close to everything here, even the famous Ward Theatre, if you so inclined to go dey, and dem have all kind'a shop on King Street."

My mother climbed down from the back of the cart. Pushcarts wove in and out of the crowds, brightly dressed higglers shouted at passersby, barefoot children squatted on the sidewalk selling fruit alongside their parents, and East Indian families sold pastry and sugarcane. She peered into the doors of well-stocked grocery shops and was greeted with smiles by eager Chinese merchants. She had never seen so many people in one place.

Because she had no fixed destination, that garden at Parade was where she slept, huddled under a thick bush with her little bundle those first few nights. She rose early, set out on foot, drank from a public standpipe, then ate one of the fruit she brought. She hoped that prospective employers, on seeing her, would not think her slim wrists inadequate for heavy lifting and sweeping, and her legs too slender for standing long hours at stoves, ironing boards, and while waiting at tables.

* * * * *

She was scrupulously looked over by the Coloured mistresses of each household, their critical eyes inspecting her smooth ebony skin, her sleek black hair, and her thick-lashed, downcast eyes. Thus scrutinized, she was deemed unemployable.

Finally, in desperation after two weeks, my mother, who was fourteen years old, turned to begging. In her wanderings, she met a watery-eyed, old brown-skinned woman in rags, named Matilda, who took up a daily post not far from the entrance to the Ward Theatre. She sold what she called Asham, which was a curious mixture of parched ground corn and spices, packaged in small pieces of old newspaper. Eager for conversation, the old woman painfully eased herself over to where my mother stood gazing at the garden and spoke urgently.

"Gal," she said, "I only hope you is not one of dem people who fool fool and think dem can live free in a dis ya garden dem 'cause if you know what I know, it overrun with criminal. Especially nighttime. Even I, who is a old woman, am 'fraid of dem 'cause dem don't care. Dem rob everybody, and beat dem up. God help you, gal, you is young. Dem will rape you. You should see the carousing that g'wan here. I lucky to have a place to sleep on Luke Lane at night."

On hearing this, my mother realized that she could no longer sleep under the bush in the garden, knowing she was vulnerable to thieves, pickpockets, and rapists.

"An' another thing," said the old woman, "You see this theatre where me standing, wid it pretty window dem and arches, an the balcony dem? It nice, eh? Well, is a British colonel name Ward who give it to we Jamaicans. Him say is a gift, an' him get it build close to Parade, 'cause dat is where dem used to drill dem soldiers. But bad thing dem always used to happen round here. Is too bad, poor people like we can't go dis ya theatre. Is only the backra them with dem nice clothes can go dey. Dem'a always tell me to g'alang, but me not moving. Not even Colonel Ward himself could'a get me leave, 'cause is here me make me living."

In her search for sanctuary, my mother occasionally found camaraderie among poor transient market people, who slept exposed to the elements in back streets. She was not always welcomed, though, since some of the folk, who were less than liberal-minded, were suspicious of her presence.

One afternoon, she roamed into the downtown tourist area near the affluent Myrtle Bank Hotel, a large, imposing building with picturesque windows and a well-groomed garden with ornate palm trees. It reminded her of a fairy-tale palace. She stood in awe, overwhelmed by its beauty, barely breathing.

"Don't mek you eye pop out," a bicyclist shouted, seeing her

4

standing there, enthralled. "Is only rich people, and well-off sick people able to go there."

Surely the compassionate must also go there, my mother must have thought, for with that in mind, she went and stood near the front entrance, with an outstretched hand.

With her poverty-stricken appearance, crumpled clothes, and bare feet, she was considered an eyesore and quickly driven away.

Despondent, she walked toward the waterfront where the sea, a rich aquamarine and silver, sparkled in the sun. Steamships were in the harbour, and a small ragtag group of half-naked boys waved at them from alongside rows of dark warehouses and import/export offices. In the distance, low stone walls restrained the restless sea as pelicans sought fish in the shallows and white gulls flew across the broad, bright sky.

She was not alone, for besides the company of ragged boys, many British and American soldiers were on shore leave. My mother, unaware that there was a war in Europe, was mesmerized by foreign sightseers carrying picnic lunches and souvenirs, while sweaty, black-skinned dock workers strained their broad backs, loading and unloading cargo in the burning sun. A few local vendors sold fruit, pastry, and handicrafts.

She climbed down a sandy bank not far from the dock, noticing pink and white shells on the narrow beach, and sat on the pale brown sand and contemplated her future before choosing a small pinkish shell as a good luck charm. Standing with her toes in the balmy waters, she watched the white-capped tide going in and out. She could not remember ever being so hungry, for back in St. Mary, there were always fruit trees and perhaps a stick of sugar cane. She was wet to her waist from the seawater before she realized it, and went to stand against the seawall. Her thin cotton skirt clung to her in the hot breeze, revealing a skeletal frame. Strangers approached and furtively pressed a halfpenny into her outstretched hand. She was unaware of the sidelong glances and blatant stares aimed at her. Overhead, scavenger John Crow birds sailed silently on their great black wings, and from hiding places beneath the dock, she heard the pew-pew cry of small hungry swallows.

* * * * *

My mother, like many of Kingston's poor, slept in crowded, makeshift shelters downtown, near busy Coronation Market or on the cold concrete of shop piazzas and abandoned sheds along back streets. She was as destitute as all those others who scavenged for food in the city dumps or begged along the city's streets. Some of them, like herself, were unaware that there was an almshouse known locally as the "poor house," which served the elderly by providing food, medicine, and lodging. But even the almhouse was already overflowing with the elderly, the sick, and the destitute.

One night in the shelter, a reedy fifteen-year-old black-skinned boy named Dudley James, who prowled the dumps by day, noticed my mother. Dudley, no stranger to the dangers of the streets, struck up conversation with her.

"If you keep going down to them wharves," he warned, "you going end up a whore. Some of we in Kingston call them 'Ladies of the Night.' It dangerous 'cause with all them sailor man wandering round with money, them bound to attract criminals. Mark my words. You could end up dead, or you could start look like old woman long before you time. It not funny, so don't laugh. Believe me, you don't want that kind'a life. And I know what I talking 'bout."

"That won't happen to me," my mother said. "Is only beg I beg, nothing else." But Dudley James was speaking from experience. He had seen many poverty-stricken young women fall victim to the allure of prostitution, and resolved to protect her. Something of her simplicity touched him, and he treated her as though she was the little sister he never had even though he could not persuade her to give up her begging post. She claimed that her occupation was "clean work," as opposed to his as a scavenger. As a compromise, he extracted a promise from her to meet him at the end of each day on crowded King Street, where homeward-bound working people would render them anonymity as they shared their meagre spoils.

My mother never knew that Dudley James lost his mother to prostitution, and that he stayed up half the night watching over her. Nor was she aware of how exhausting his days were as he and other street urchins scavenged in the sweltering sun. And she knew nothing about the fist fights and quarrels over items they found, some of which could be sold, used, or eaten. Dudley kept his bruises hidden, and never spoke of his past.

One hot night, a loud commotion in the shelter awakened my mother. She immediately noticed that Dudley was not beside her. She heard loud terrified screams and moans, and the unmistakable sound of bodies thrashing. Women were being molested in the dark, while terrified weeping children huddled fearfully in the shadows. A gang of men had broken in, intent on robbery and rape, but were unsuccessful at silencing the occupants. A small kerosene lamp hanging near the entrance cast violent, grotesque shadows on the thin walls and frightened my mother. She saw Dudley on the other side of the room, which was little more than a structure of crocus bags and cardboard. He was wounded, and had been trying to protect her. A gash near his temple oozed thick blood down his cheek, and his clothes and hands were splattered. "Dudley!" she screamed, forgetting her own safety as she scrambled toward him. On seeing her, he backed off.

"Go!" he shouted. "I'm alright."

"Dudley, you not alright! You bleeding!"

"Run," he shouted, "before they rape you!"

My mother hesitated, but he was insistent. Then out of the darkness, one of the hooligans made a grab for her. "You naw going get way," he hissed. But Dudley, who was lithe and muscular, seized the culprit in a headlock and held him fast, giving my mother an opportunity to escape.

She never looked back as she ran barefoot down the long, gloomy, garbage-strewn lane adjacent to the market, holding her threadbare skirt high. She could still hear the sound of the distant commotion, even as the sleepy lane erupted with its own noises. Insects droned loudly, poultry squawked, and dogs yapped fiercely behind fences. In her flight, she tripped over protruding stones in the dirt and stubbed her toes in unexpected holes before falling more than once. Then, remembering the lucky shell she had tied around her waist in her thread bag, she quickly got up, ignoring her bruises, and kept going.

Though exhausted, she clambered over a low fence and ducked in and out of side streets until she found herself in a residential backyard. A thick bougainvillea hedge ran the length of the yard. She peered through the hedge and in the moonlight saw a horse tethered not far from a garage. The garage doors were open. She forced her way through the bushes, forgetting that there might be a watchdog on the property. However, there was no resulting alarm when she emerged from the hedge. It was only when she heard loud voices from somewhere close by that she lost her nerve. She crouched low and ran pell-mell between the horse's legs toward the garage. The horse barely moved a muscle or made a sound besides snorting as she quickly pulled the garage doors shut behind her.

Despite the dimness inside, there was no mistaking the large black buggy parked there. She had seen it many times on King Street when its owners, Mr. and Mrs. Wayne Arlington, went shopping for millinery supplies. Mrs. Arlington was particularly fond of fine lace and broad, expensively adorned hats, and her husband thought nothing of indulging her. She considered herself a cut above the other White English upper-class families in Kingston because her husband, Wayne, was assistant to the

King's representative on the island. She would have been shocked had she known of my mother's presence in her garden. How often had she said that she could never accustom herself to living among the illiterate and misinformed Negroes on the island. She had even brought an Englishman to serve as their watchman, unaware that he was partial to rum-drinking binges, then sleeping it off through the long evenings in a crawl space under the veranda. His carelessness was evident in his leaving the garage doors wide open.

Without hesitation, my mother slid under the low-slung buggy, praying that the frantic drumming of her heart would not betray her. She could hear the raucous voices and the running feet in pursuit. She covered her mouth, willed herself to remain calm, and strained her ears, listening. Hours passed slowly for her beneath the buggy, and it was almost dawn when there were sounds of roosters crowing and a lone donkey braying.

She emerged cautiously from her hiding place. Fearful of being charged with trespassing, she crept out of the garage, noticing for the first time the stately home beyond the garage with its intricately carved railings, columns, and broad veranda. To her surprise, she noticed a pair of feet clad in black leather shoes sticking out from the underside of the veranda. Though partially obscured by an oleander bush and thick grass, there was no mistaking the watchman's uniform. My mother immediately ran, fearing reprisals.

Covered in dust, she furtively made her way through the back streets, unsure of her destination. She was in a busy lane, for pushcarts rumbled by and early rising higglers with baskets on their heads hurried toward Parade. Up ahead, she made out the figure of an old woman. It was Matilda, who sold Asham near the Ward Theatre. Matilda approached her cautiously, leaning heavily on a stick.

"Is you that?" Matilda inquired, her eyes watering as she slowly drew abreast to peer into my mother's tired eyes. "Me did think it was you, but me couldn'a be sure. Last night me couldn'a sleep. Such a ruckus was'a go on. Woman and man dem a' scream, an me hear a boy named Dudley beat up so bad, him mus'be dead. Me don't know much, but dem say police come tek him away 'cause him bleed all night. You alright, gal? Is long time me don't see you. A'what me did tell you, long time gone, badness walks these streets." My mother's head swam with the information.

"Where them take him?" she asked, already afraid of the old woman's answer. Sensing her distress, Matilda placed a scrawny freckled hand on my mother's shoulder.

"You mean you don't know that we poor people always end up in'a Kingston Public Hospital? If him alive, that is where him is, but if him dead, him would'a end up in'a May Pen Cemetery."

My mother was never to see Dudley James again.

*****

My mother returned to the waterfront that afternoon, after spending most of the morning frantically peering through the low windows of the Kingston Public Hospital. She caught glimpses of bandaged patients asleep in sunny wards filled with long rows of metal beds and various medical paraphernalia. There were overpowering fumes from disinfectants, carbolic soap, and gangrene. She was reluctant to make inquiries, intimidated by the long lines of the injured, diseased, and dying, and knew instinctively that, in spite of her wretchedness, she would not get attention from the busy medical practitioners.

Dudley will send word if he is able to, she thought, consoling herself.

The waterfront was particularly busy that afternoon. A peanut vendor entertained passersby with an old black doll that popped out from a sack. Two men played on a fife and whistle, sharing a hat for begging between them. Not far off, sailors listened to a small calypso band, while vendors enticed them with pastry, cheap toys, and souvenirs.

My mother didn't make a penny that day, though she lingered until the ladies of the night came out late in the evening to escort willing sailors.

The moon was out and the sea, a sheet of blackened glass, reflected the starlit sky. My mother's eyes were heavy with sleep, and her stomach growled from hunger when she finally turned to face the dark, brooding city. Near the end of the wharf, a figure, half obscured by the night, silently stepped out and stood in front of her. It was one of the ladies of the night. She was quite dark-skinned and attractive, wearing fake gold bracelets and a long, revealing flimsy dress that fell to her ankles. Her coarse hair was covered with a long scarf. "Where you going, little girl?" she asked, her red lips bright against the dark as the heavy scent of Kus Kus perfume and cigarettes wafted around her.

"I want to get some sleep," my mother replied.

"Is sleep you want? You did look so sad, me did think you lost. Well, since is only dat, come wid me. Don't be 'fraid. Me naw go hurt you."

My mother, naïve and exhausted, followed the strange woman along the deserted wharf. A cool wind blew off the glassy sea. White spray spread like fingers below the dock, and the warehouses loomed in the moonlight.

"Bend down low," the woman whispered, stopping momentarily to lift aside a couple of loose planks on the side of the closest warehouse. "We going inside. Come quick, before the stupid night watchman dem come."

The interior was pitch black, though moonlight glimmered through cracks in the wood. Wooden boxes, crates, and jute sacks were haphazardly piled throughout the room, barely catching the light.

"Hold me hand," the woman said. "You don't want to get lost. It big in here, and it easy to buck up on the thing dem. You'll get used to it. You can lie down and sleep beside dis carton box. Don't move 'cause other people in here. Them won't bother you. But I have to go back out, so stay here till I get back."

Left alone in the dark, my mother heard coughs, snores, wheezes, and low murmurings. Rats scurried among paper and sawdust shavings, and the stench of urine, feces, stale alcohol, and vomit was overwhelming. She lay quite still in a fetal position on the dingy floor until cramps set in. She stretched her hand out and felt something brush lightly against her fingers. She froze, for what ever it was tried to crawl into her palm, and then she saw that it was a large cockroach. Breaking into a cold sweat, she sprang up.

"Oh Lord, get me out of here!" she cried out loudly, forgetting that she was not alone. Within minutes, she heard shuffling coming from the far side of the warehouse, followed by heavy footsteps and urgent whispering. She tried desperately to squeeze herself behind the carton box. She drew her knees tightly up to her chest, trying to make herself smaller, and waited with damp cheeks, hoping that somehow the dimness would hide her and keep predators at bay.

"Who is it?" she asked feebly, feeling the toe of a hard boot next to her cheek. But there was no answer. Several pairs of rough hands grabbed her, and a dirty sack reeking of dust and rat droppings was quickly shoved over her head and her hands were tied. She tried to scream, but to no avail, for her mouth was brutally covered by a large hand, and her saliva was thick with dust and jute debris. Her attackers made no more than muffled sounds as they systematically ripped off her clothes. She could smell the stench of body odours, chewing tobacco, and cheap rum.

My mother never spoke of the poignant events that occurred the day after she was raped, nor the weeks of illness that led to the discovery of her pregnancy. She only confided that it was fear that made her abandon the waterfront to solicit along North Street, which was further uptown.

CHAPTER 2

Madam Hung Chin

*H*oly Trinity Cathedral, the most spectacular building on North Street, was built in 1911, a few years after the earthquake in Kingston. It is imposing, not only as a result of its Revival Byzantine style, its massive eighty-foot, copper-lined dome and four minarets, but also because of its massive pipe organ. It was there that Jesuit priests who taught at the nearby St. George's Catholic School officiated at Mass. Father Gabriel O'Sullivan, a seventy-five-year-old priest from Boston, was one of them. His passion was service to the poor and devotion to Our Lady of Sorrows. In spite of age and arthritic knees, he cultivated a habit he called "scouring." He laboriously limped along North Street as he sought out the poor, the mentally ill, the sick, and the destitute to offer food, clothing, referrals to charitable agencies, and Holy Communion.

When first he saw my mother, she was wearing rags and appeared waif-like. Her thin cheekbones stood out gaunt against her hollow eyes, and her lips were dried and scaled from hunger. Her ripening stomach, which had begun to show, protruded like a grapefruit on a slender branch. Father O'Sullivan felt pity and approached her.

"My child," he said, "your life is hard, but be assured, God has not forgotten you. I'm a priest from Holy Trinity Cathedral. I feel certain that it is God's will and the urgent prayers of our Mother Mary, who loves all mothers, that has brought you here. I will see to it that you are given a bit to eat and a drop of something to drink."

Father O'Sullivan's gentle manner and kindness brought tears, and the small meal of codfish and rice he provided her in the church rectory prompted more. It was the first of many meals, for Father O'Sullivan saw to it that she was among those in the line-ups at the rectory twice a week when he himself ladled out meagre meals and milk to the needy.

Scanty though those meals were, they were my mother's lifeline. One day, in her eighth month of pregnancy, when she went as usual to Holy Trinity Cathedral, she saw other poor people standing around, looking despondent and grumbling among themselves. She walked past them, right up to the rectory door, and knocked timidly. A broad-hipped, tired-looking middle-aged woman wearing a white cap and apron answered.

"I is Rita, the housekeeper," the woman said. "Look, if is food you look for, Father O'Sullivan not here no more. Him get transfer. Them send him to a country parish, in St. James, so him can take it easy in him old age. We not going be able to give out no more food 'cause Father used to buy such things out of money him get from family donations in America. But with America in the war, that money not going come here no more."

"No food." My mother sighed, feeling hunger claw at her gut, and not for a moment realizing the enormity of a world war. "What I going do?"

The housekeeper smiled weakly. "You better go ask you baby father for help."

My mother resumed begging along North Street, hoping desperately that Father O'Sullivan might return. Occasionally, she was given a penny by strangers, and she felt lucky when one day

14

a little girl gave her a mango. She feared returning to sleep in shelters at night, and cultivated the habit of sleeping underneath residential houses in the area. Whenever she chose a house, she always made sure that there were no watchdogs, and that not too many people came and went, and she tried not to sleep under the same house twice.

One morning, after having slept under one of these houses, she emerged into the sunlight with cobweb-strewn hair. She brushed off her clothes, ran fingers through her hair, and quite unexpectedly experienced a sharp cramp in her side. She dragged herself out of the fenced yard, through a side gate, and was out on the road when she saw a bank of small yellow wildflowers. She sat down among them, catching her breath, wondering what would become of her and her child. She noticed a house across the street with a hedge of bright red hibiscus. She was hungry and thirsty, and the house looked welcoming. She rose with much effort, crossed the street, and used a pebble to knock on the house's metal gates.

"Beg you piece of bread," she called out, her voice at first only a whisper, then turned louder as she experienced unaccustomed twinges and pain in her abdomen.

A child no older than my mother came down the hibiscus-lined walkway, bringing water in a rough enamel cup, the type usually reserved for use by servants and others in the lower classes. My mother accepted the cup with a trembling hand, and did not mention to the child about how her legs ached or how her temples pounded. She drank noisily, wiping small beads of sweat from her forehead. When she returned the cup, a woman who must have been the child's mother came out on to the veranda and called to the child.

"Effie, give this to her. The poor thing must be starving."

My mother stood at the gate, willing herself not to collapse in spite of nausea and dizziness as she placed her trembling hands on her bulging belly for support. The child handed her a thick slice of bread, which she ate hungrily. The woman spontaneously reached into her pocket, retrieved a shilling, and came down to the gate to hand it to my mother, whispering, "God Bless."

Carrying the shilling in the thread bag, my mother walked toward Parade. She had not seen the old woman Matilda in months, and wondered if she might know what to do about the pain. She was in a lane when she heard higglers and market women laughing and talking loudly. Suddenly embarrassed by her condition, she ducked behind a zinc fence and watched the women go by, burdened down with produce. The pain was getting harder to ignore. She came out from her hiding place, noticing a small shop close by. Perhaps milk will settle me, she thought.

The small grocery shop was on Luke Lane, not far from a row of garment manufacturers. She crossed the road and mounted the piazza. The dingy, dimly lit shop was not unlike other buildings on the lane, with its hand-lettered sign over the door, which read "Chin's Grocery."

Once inside, she looked around at the sparsely stocked shelves, the jars of candy paradise plums and mint balls, as well as pieces of dried salted codfish on the counter, where a swarm of small flies hung in the air, attracted by a dish of Blackie mangoes. At first she did not notice Madam Hung Chin, the Chinese shop-keeper, who was sitting on a low stool, occupied with scooping out and sorting portions of rice to sell by weight. When Madam rose to weigh the rice on a metal scale, her sudden appearance startled my mother.

"Morning," Madam said, a wide grin wrinkling her thin, skull-like face. "What you like today?"

"Milk," my mother replied feebly.

"Condense or cow's?"

"Cow's."

"You have money?"

"Yes."

"Good, I'll get milk from back."

Though Madam Hung Chin must have been in her late sixties, her steps were as light as a child's and her movements sure and quick. The slippers she wore were faded with Chinese designs, and her hair, though dark, had a few grey strands.

No sooner had Madam left the room when my mother's water broke. Petrified, she stood in the puddle, feeling helpless and ashamed. The pains became more frequent, and she felt as though her entire interior had been ripped open by a cutlass.

"Help!" she screamed, collapsing on the wooden floor, writhing and sweating profusely. Madam came running, dropping the rag she had been wiping off the milk bottle with and, without hesitation, squatted down and gently held my mother's head in her lap, stroking her hair and using the hem of her skirt to wipe away my mother's beads of sweat.

"What you name, girl?"

"Margaret."

"Well, Margaret, you baby coming. No one else here, so is me you going trust. I going put this small flat flour sack under you head, so I can go close shop door. Nobody to upset you, okay?"

"Yes."

"Don't worry, I deliver many babies in China."

Madam was so reassuring that my mother felt safe, though she moaned, screamed, and cried out loudly from the intense pain. Madam Hung Chin spread clean flour bags on the floor and gently lifted my mother, first an arm, then a leg, onto the sacks, and placed a small flat flour sack under my mother's head. She squatted on the floor between my mother's legs and removed my mother's underwear.

"It coming!" she shouted triumphantly. "I see the head. You going to have to push!"

"Oh my God," my mother cried out, breathing heavily, more terrified than ever.

"Margaret, I going to grab the baby shoulders to help it come, alright?"

"Anything … just stop the pain."

"Look, Margaret, look—see you fine baby boy. Is what you going to call him?"

Propping herself up on her elbows, my mother peered at the baby covered in blood and birthing fluids, and was transformed by the perfection of its tiny face, its hands and feet.

"Him beautiful, but I never thought of a name. Will you name him for me?"

Madam Hung Chin smiled. "Call him John. It was me husband's English name. And look how the baby look so white—him must be English."

* * * * *

"You want me send go get the baby father?"

"No … don't know who the father is."

"What you mean?"

"T'was rape. Them cover me head."

"Strangers them?"

"Yes."

"Poor soul. What about you mother and father?"

"Them dead."

"You don't have nobody?"

"Nobody."

"Where you stay?"

"Nowhere."

"Good Lord! You going have to stay then. I clear out stockroom, alright? Not much stock anyway. See?"

"You is very kind, an' I don't want to be ungrateful, but … I can't pay."

"No need pay. Just help out in store when you get stronger. Such a beautiful baby need home, right? You go rest. I hold him. Him so pretty. Is almost like me is grandmother."

"What you name, lady?"

"Me? My name is Hung Chin. Just call me Madam, like everybody else."

"Thank you, Madam, you is godsend."

* * * * *

My first memories are of the open yard behind Madam Hung Chin's shop. I can still recall how good it felt to run on my short legs past bush and burrs, with wind in my hair, sunlight warm on my skin, and the assurance that if I fell, Madam would catch me.

"Don't want you to ever hurt," she would say over and over, patting my hair and setting me upright. Whenever my mother helped out in the shop, I had Madam all to myself, and even though I was only three, she took me for walks, pointing out plants and weeds useful for teas and healing.

"Sorrel good for iron, garlic good for blood pressure, rosehip make soothing tea, and thyme good for sore throat." Sometimes I can almost hear her still.

"An see that building beside me shop? You mustn't go over dey. Is Syrian people factory. Dem might think you is one of dem and steal you. All the building dem belong to Jew and Syrian. Is only the rum shop man in the next lane Chinese like me. Me heart would break if you lost."

On birthdays, Madam hoisted me up on the shop counter, telling everyone about my special day, and she was more than delighted when some of her poverty-stricken customers would return with a little something for me. One woman brought a handkerchief, another brought an avocado pear, a boy left half of his bulla cake, and an old man in rags left a tin cup he himself had hammered out.

How joyful those days were as Mamma and I and Madam drank condensed milk in celebration of my birthday. The sweetness still lingers on my lips. On those nights, after the shop was closed, Madam Hung Chin would pull out a wind-up victrola from under a stack of boxes to play wondrous Chinese waltzes. The foreign music floated in the squalid room, and she would be transformed. The music spoke eloquently of waterfalls, emperors, palaces, loneliness, peasants, and poverty, and now and again it would seductively affirm the promise that love lost could be regained. Madam, with tears in her eyes, would say, "Let's dance, Baby John." She let me stand on top of her slippered feet and we waltzed, oblivious to time and untouched by events to come. How I loved those moments, for it was as though the haunting music was part of myself, and the sound of Madam's soft sobbing was my own sweet tears.

* * * * *

"How come you baby so white? Him look Jew. Is who him father?"

A group of black-skinned young women were at the shop counter idling, as Madam would say. One of them was pestering my mother about me, and Mamma, not noticing me come up behind her, kept talking.

"Ramona, how I going know who him father is? I get rape down at the waterfront."

"Well, darling, you boy must be a sailor man pickney, for all of us can see that him hair straight, him skin light, and him eye them greyish."

"Ramona, it don't matter that him don't look like me, 'cause I love him same way."

"But, Margaret, you should try find him daddy. You couldn'a get money, you know. If it was me, that sucker would'a have to pay, and if is White man, better still. All a dem have money."

* * * * *

As a result of that conversation, my mother began to frequent the waterfront again, never saying where she was going, and always leaving just after her chores in the shop were finished. Madam, more than delighted to have me in her care, never asked her where she went.

In my mother's absence, Madam would teach me strange Chinese words, repeating the sounds over and over until I got them right. Then she would take out the abacus she used in the store and teach me the rudiments of addition and subtraction, all the while pretending that it was just a game.

"Take ten dog, put them over here. Come, Baby John, count out the bead dem. Good. Okay, that make ten. Three dog run 'way. How many dog left to bite you? Count the bead them. Good boy, you going real smart. Me husband did smart too."

"Where him is, Madam?"

"Him did go back'a China 'cause we money over dey. Them say him ship sink in'a the war. But I wait here, case him not dead."

"Will he bring us more music?"

"Yes, everything will be better ... and not just for me, but you too."

*****

I was four years old when the bad news came. I was playing on the property at the back of the clothing manufacturer next door, having not heeded Madam's warning. Two local boys, Leslie and Errol, who were slightly older than I, had managed to shimmy over the wood fence that separated it from Madam's yard. We were among barrels and boxes of discarded scraps of fabric when a man's voice shouted my name. The urgency in his voice startled me. I tried to run, but Errol and Leslie bolted, leaving me stranded as they squeezed through an opening in the back fence.

"John!" the voice boomed again. My legs were too short, and I couldn't catch up with the others. I looked up to see a fair-skinned man running toward me. I couldn't move. I was frozen to the spot, for surely this man with sandy hair was certain to be one of the Jews or Syrians Madam had said would steal me! I could barely breathe. There was no escape.

"John!" the man shouted. "Don't be afraid. Madam sent me. Look, John, she is in front of the building. She needs you. Come, little man, don't cry."

Mr. Costa, the owner of the manufacturing company, wasn't lying. Madam was at the front of the building. I had never seen her look so upset and distraught.

"I won't go over there again," I sobbed, eager to placate her. But she stood in the lane, looking strangely lost and hunched over. I wondered if she knew I was there. Her eyes were tightly closed, and when she opened them, I saw tears.

"Come, Baby John," she said huskily, reaching for me to bury my head in the hollow of her thin shoulders. "Is only me you have now," she added softly. "You mother dead."

Holding tightly to my small hand, Madam Hung Chin began marching toward the waterfront. I remember how stunned I was, unable to fully comprehend what death meant. Every step of the way, Madam, holding her head high, was joined by neighbours, curiosity seekers, and shop customers, not to mention Mr. Costa himself. What a curious party we made.

The fragrant scent of the sea, heavy in the air, and the sound of our collective footfalls are etched in my memory. Low voices murmured, then whispered, argued, and quarrelled, growing to crescendo as each of the marchers speculated on my mother's fate.

"Her time must'a come," was one woman's theory, but she was hushed into silence by the others.

"Her time cut short," said another.

We arrived at the wharf to find a larger crowd already congregated, jostling for more advantageous positions to observe the solemn activities taking place on the narrow beach below, where my mother's body lay perfectly still, covered with a white cotton cloth. Ten policemen, with the help of a few civilians, were trying to keep the crowds away. Medical examiners stood near the body, shaking their heads knowingly and taking notes.

"Her son is here!" A dishevelled old man cried out loudly, noticing our arrival. He was the old man who had at one time given me a tin cup. The crowd collectively turned to stare at us. And I, filled with fear, did not notice how they delighted in how my hair glinted saffron in the sun, and how ruddy my cheeks were against my grey eyes.

"Is her son that?" One of the men inquired incredulously.

"Yes, is her son," Madam Hung Chin shouted, holding my hand ever more tightly. "I know, 'cause I myself deliver him."

"Well, ask him if this is him mother," said a policeman. "Pass him over here to us."

Without further warning, I was passed hands over heads, and felt like a rubber ball bobbing on water. From that vantage, I marvelled at the stark white clouds, and saw the tide rush with brute force to where my mother lay on the gravelly beach, and I prayed it would touch her gently and waken her from her dreaming.

Down on the beach, one of the policemen held me high on his shoulders, while another peeled away my mother's shroud, and I saw her. Her smooth velvet skin, her laughing eyes now closed, and her whole countenance settled into unaccustomed gravity, as though finally at peace.

"Mamma!" I gasped as the policemen sedately nodded their heads.

"She was stabbed to death." The policeman holding me addressed a colleague. "It might have been a botched robbery attempt, because this was found not far from the body."

I realized then that he had been gripping something in his hand, and when he lifted it up, I saw that it was the pouch containing my mother's lucky shell.

* * * * *

23

It was a warm January day when my mother was laid to rest in a pauper's grave in May Pen Cemetery. Her murderer was never caught, and she was not to know that a conference for world peace had taken place in Versailles, France, and that in June of that year the Treaty of Versailles would be signed, ending the war. And she had not foreseen that I would be left as sole companion to Madam Hung Chin.

"Times hard," Madam said one evening. "We not getting much stock from foreign, even though some of we Jamaican soldier dem did go a'war. We going have to tighten we belts."

"What them was fighting 'bout, Madam?"

"A whole lot a thing, Baby John, but some bad people want colony in Africa, an' power in China, and them secretly have big army dem in Europe that get too powerful, and England and America go in war against them. Many, many people dead. Them had machine gun. We lucky we over here."

"You frighten, Madam?"

"Yes, 'cause war can come back again."

CHAPTER 3

Myths and Legends

W hen I was five, Madam Hung Chin sent me to a Chinese school, located on South Camp Road, on the upper floor of an ornate, two-storey, Victorian-style house. The rooms were airy and spacious, though the walls crumbled into a powdery white dust when we poked our pencils into cracks. The hardwood floors sagged, and our every step resulted in audible creaks. Over in a corner, near the largest window that overlooked the garden, was an old black piano with keys that reminded me of yellowed teeth. It was donated by a British missionary who had at one time lived in China. The piano boasted a small gold-plated placard that read "This piano is lovingly donated to the Chinese Children of Jamaica by the Rev. Wilton Staples. May it bring music to their lives." Those solemn words, which we read over and over, served as a reminder of his generosity. Our teacher, Miss Wang, a tight-jawed, young Chinese woman with fierce black eyes, played monotonous sharp notes that grated against our high voices as we recited the alphabet and repeated math drills. I was the only one of her eight students who was not Chinese.

"What it matter if he only one not Chinese?" Madam Hung

Chin used to say when asked about it. "He live with me, and I Chinese."

The school was originally intended for Chinese immigrant children learning English, but because of declining enrolment, the occasional non-Chinese child was accepted.

The first floor of the house was mysterious to me. The curtains were always drawn, and we never saw the occupants, though we were constantly reminded to be quiet so as not to disturb them. Madam Hung Chin told me that they were White people, and that I should avoid contact with them, for she was certain that a fair-haired child, such as I was, would easily assimilate, and undoubtedly she would never see me again.

The wide windows on the second floor where the classroom was were framed in dark mahogany wood and had no curtains. The rich gloss of the mahogany panels added unexpected elegance to the decaying room. There were small oak desks and chairs for each student, and metal hooks behind the broad wooden door on which to hang our satchels of supplies since the desks had no drawers. Miss Wang sat with her back to the windows, glaring at us from her own oak desk, and I imagined that her neatly stashed desk drawers were filled with work for us to do. Little did I know that Miss Wang was a devotee of Chinese romance novels, which she stored there.

The heady scent of roses wafted into the classroom through three large windows, which Miss Wang always kept opened, firmly believing in the benefits of fresh air.

"Air will stimulate brain," she said, gazing out at the beautiful garden below full of velvety red and yellow roses. At the centre of the garden was a sturdy alamander bush with flowers the colour of rich butter, bitter-tasting petals, and dark green foliage. I, too, gazed frequently at the garden, longing to escape the confines of the classroom and to be lost in its floral wilderness.

My fellow students were all related: Alfred and Sharon Lee

were brother and sister, Trevor and Paul Chung their cousins, and Elizabeth Lyn, Charmaine Yin, and the twins Rudolph and Carol Holong were related by marriage. Our ages ranged from four to six, though we were all taught the same lessons.

One morning, I arrived early with Madam and found Trevor, Rudolph, and Paul waiting on the veranda. The doors were opened at seven-thirty and never a moment earlier by Miss Wang herself. Madam Hung Chin had only just said goodbye to me and was gone when, without warning, Paul, who was four and the youngest of us, ran down the crumbling stone steps into the garden. His clothes caught on thorns, which pierced his tender skin. He cried piteously as the sharp thorns held him fast. Terrified, the rest of us were unsure of what to do. The front door suddenly opened with a bang. A tall White woman with long, curly red hair came running, and I couldn't help but think that she must have been observing us from behind the curtains.

"Boys," she called out, "you have to be careful. Rose bushes are filled with thorns. You could get hurt. Stand over here. I'll fetch him and take him inside to put something on his cuts and scrapes."

I almost fainted. Surely this woman would take me away, I thought. The other boys had no such fear, and in a minute we were all in the ground floor living room. What a room it was! Colourful Oriental rugs covered the beautiful hardwood floors, and dozens of framed photographs were atop carved dark wooden buffets and curio cabinets. A pale pink footstool stood beside an elegant cane rocking chair. Two large peach-coloured couches with wooden armrests had six huge red velvet cushions. Yellow roses from the garden, set among lacy ferns, peered out from tall cut-glass vases, but my eyes were drawn to the photographs. Lambs gambolled, dogs with long tongues sat with small, strangely dressed children, men in uniform stared unblinkingly at the camera, brides and grooms smiled wanly, and old grandmothers with severe expressions stood proudly in unfamiliar landscapes. Finally, a profile of a little girl with curls, holding a flower, was caught in sepia forever.

The filtered light from the drawn curtains gave the room a mysteriously foreign atmosphere, and the scent of roses and hidden mothballs hung heavily in the air.

"My name is Miss Fiona Shaw," the woman said, coming up quietly behind me. "I'm American. See that man in the photo with the uniform? That's my father. He was in the war, and that little girl with the curls was me when I was your age."

I turned reluctantly from the photographs, noticing that Paul's wounds had been attended to, and a small bottle of iodine had recently been placed on one of the sideboards.

"He'll be alright," the woman said, following my gaze. "No harm done." She smiled reassuringly. "However," she said, "I'm curious about you. I thought the school was for Chinese children. Do you speak Chinese?"

The other boys were quiet, as though collectively holding their breath, awaiting my reply. Not even Paul uttered a sound.

"Yes," I said softly, anxious to make it to the open door.

"What's your name?" she called after me, ignoring the others.

"John," I replied. With eyes downcast, I walked out the door to my deliverance.

* * * * *

By the time I was eight, Miss Shaw had become a familiar part of our school life. She often came upstairs to the classroom to regale us with stories. She told us about Paul Bunyan, the mighty logger, and Pecos Bill, who used a snake as a lasso, and on rainy days, we listened to rain hammering on the shingled roof as she recounted tales of Brer Rabbit, who seemed much the same as our Anancy. And all the while as she was telling us stories, she fixed her eyes on me with much curiosity.

"Tell us 'bout the cowboys and Indians in America," the Chinese children would say, and she always looked to me for approval before telling us wondrous Ojibway, Cree, and Dakota legends, seducing us with their textures, rhythms, and pacing.

One day I told Madam Hung Chin about the stories, and how Miss Shaw favoured me. Madam immediately covered her ears. She shook her head from side to side stubbornly, as though blocking my words.

"Don't listen to them stories!" she hissed. "We have own stories. My people is Hakka, from the poorest of China's eighteen provinces. Hakka woman equal to man, they not bind feet. We come from cradle of Chinese civilization near Yellow River. Big rebellion against Confucius give Hakka militant Christian religion, but we still have Chinese tradition. Hakka have secret language, too, Baby John, and many stories. We is migrant that pick up culture, so we have to work hard to be who we are."

Madam Hung Chin sounded so fiercely passionate that it frightened me.

"I tell you Hakka story, Baby John."

"I'm not a baby, Madam."

"No, but you is my baby now, eh?"

When she said that, I turned my head away, too embarrassed to face her, my heart brimming over with love.

"The story I going tell might be true, but then again, it might not, okay?"

I curled up on the coya mattress that was my bed and that had been my mother's, and Madam Hung Chin came into the room that had been her old stockroom. She clutched a red book in her hand, and the expression in her eyes had softened.

"Listen," she said solemnly, "don't ask question. The book write in English, okay?"

She needn't have said anything, for I was already all ears and eager.

* * * * *

29

A long time ago, in the poorest province in China, there lived a Hakka family. There was a father, a mother, and their twin daughters, Ching Hai and Hung Lin.

The father had been a farmer, but could no longer farm, for he was old and feeble. The mother, too, had grown old and no longer farmed. All they had left of the farm was their shack and an old ox. It was the twin daughters who brought food to their table.

Ching Hai, who loved to dance, danced outside their humble shack every day. Passing travellers who appreciated her beautiful dancing placed coins in a large blue-and-white ceramic vase she kept at the shack's door. By nightfall the vase was almost always half full.

Hung Lin, on the other hand, loved the serenity of the forest nearby, where she gathered herbs—calamus, wormwood, and cornel leaf—to sell to travellers. One day, she was alone gathering herbs when a handsome young man, the son of an emperor, was riding in the forest. Hung Lin could not take her eyes off him, for his face, his fine clothes, and the lance that he carried shone like the sun. All was quiet in the forest as though nature itself had stopped to admire him. All of a sudden, a ferocious wild bear came out from its cave and frightened the young man's horse. The young man drew his lance and killed the bear, but in doing so, he was thrown from his horse and was injured.

With all the strength she had, Hung Lin dragged the young man into the bear's cave, and cared for him there for many days, using herbs and potions. After a month of her vigilance, he was stronger. She helped him onto his horse and bound him into his saddle with strong wild vines.

"I bind you with love," she whispered as she secured him. Then she got her family's one ox and rode on its back to accompany the young man and his horse to his distant province.

The people of his kingdom rejoiced at the young man's safe return, and when he proposed marriage to the girl on the ox, they celebrated, all except for the emperor, who resented the girl's poverty and ordered her to leave his son. Heartbroken and unmarried, Hung Lin returned to her own province, where she lived in the forest's isolation.

Many years passed, the emperor died, and his son, the young man, managed to find his way back to Hung Lin's village. Passing by her shack, he saw her twin sister dancing in front of the dwelling. Thinking it was Hung Lin, he fell in love all over again, and planned to marry the dancing girl.

News of her sister's impending marriage reached Hung Lin in the forest, and she returned home to offer her blessing. On seeing the beautiful girl with potions and herbs hanging from her belt, the young man realized his mistake. Ching Hai, too, realized that it was Hung Lin who had saved the prince's life, and that Hung Lin was the person the young man was in love with. She no longer danced, her heart was too sad, she sought refuge in the forest, and took a rough woven mat with her to sleep on.

The mat she slept on was found days later soaked in blood and tears. Only a small golden heart embedded in the fabric was testament to her love. Ching Hai had either killed herself, or was eaten by a wild beast.

The rich young man married Hung Lin years later in the rocky Guangdong region of China, and it is said to this day that Hung Lin wears a small gold heart at her throat.

* * * * *

"Was that a true story, Madam?"
"Who knows, Baby John."
"What was you name in China, Madam?"
"Hung Lin."

31

"Are you wearing a gold heart, Madam?"
"Yes, but tell me, you like story?"
"Yes."
"You can have the book then, Baby John."

CHAPTER 4

News from Abroad

*A*s Madam Hung Chin grew older, she reverted to speaking only in Hakka when we were alone, and grew unaccustomedly impatient if I didn't get words right. We used to sit in our airless kitchen, its walls almost as black as the coal stove she perched her wok on.

"House is vo," she said pointing all over the room. "Talk is gong." Then she would take a spoonful of rice from her bowl and chew quickly. "Eat is sit fan."

"Say word again, John, one more time. You mustn't forget. You mustn't forget things I teach you."

The problem was not in my forgetting, it was that Madam herself had started experiencing memory loss and, try as she might, her mind slowed as her hair grew rapidly whiter and her eyelids drooped into folds of wrinkled skin, giving her a permanent squint.

"Madam, school taking us to pantomime at Ward Theatre tomorrow."

"Why you don't tell me before, John?"

"I told you last week."

"Oh, sorry, I forget. We have to pay?"

"No, Madam, it's a treat from Miss Shaw. She say we need to know Jamaican culture."

"Miss Shaw, Miss Shaw, all I ever hear is Miss Shaw. No wonder I have bad headache."

"Did you have some Chinese tea?"

"No, it not going to help, but know what, John? Let we dance 'cause day after tomorrow is you birthday."

"I know, Madam. Can't we dance on the birthday as usual?"

"John, we might be busy, okay? Anyway, John, you make Hakka noodle. For life of me, can't remember recipe."

Though Madam was smiling bravely, I knew something was terribly wrong. How could she forget something she did every day? I nervously hummed a tune familiar to us both, and reached across the table to take her frail hand in mine.

"How old you are, Madam?"

"Me? I'm eighty-two, and you is going to be ten in two days. You no longer baby."

I got up from my seat, and stood beside Madam. She stood up, too, and I drew her to my breast. I was already taller than she was, for she must have shrunken. I felt her weary heart beating against my chest, like a frightened swallow with a broken wing.

"Let's dance, Madam," I said, and together we waltzed in that tiny kitchen, with its cracked windowpanes, my heart beating as rapidly as hers, and hoping that my youth and strength could somehow sustain her.

* * * * *

"What you going put in Hakka noodles, John?" Madam asked, her once-strong voice trembling and fearful. "Tell me, John, mustn't forget, or something bad might happen."

"I have everything we need, Madam. Don't worry, I won't forget."

"John, you is young, memory sharp. Thank God. What you have there?"

"Madam," I said slowly, "I have the flat noodles, chillies, scallion, sweet pepper, garlic, vinegar, salt, and the yellow food colouring, plus oil to fry everything in."

"You learn quick, John. We eat good tonight."

Madam had no recall that Hakka noodles was something she had shown me how to cook twice a day, every day, for the last six years.

＊＊＊＊＊

I awoke early the next morning, anxious to attend the pantomime with my classmates, their parents, and Madam Hung Chin, but I found Madam sitting up in her bed. She looked as faded as the dishcloths in the kitchen, and she had tied a damp rag around her head.

"Can't come with you, John. Headache very bad today. You go alone. I take easy, okay?"

Seeing the look of disappointment in my eyes, she called me over.

"Sit beside me, John. I want see you smile. Madam love you. Know what? I give you early birthday present. I pull victrola out last night. It for you, John. It make you happy, yes?"

"You sure, Madam? I mean about the victrola."

"Yes."

"Thanks, Madam. Tomorrow will be my best birthday. Want some green tea?"

"Not now, John. When you get back. Just need rest. Love you, Baby John."

"Love you too."

＊＊＊＊＊

It wasn't to be my best birthday. I raced home from the Ward Theatre that afternoon, thrilled by the performance, the lights, the hand-painted set, the wonderful columns, and the dimly lit balcony where we sat, feeling like royalty, as we looked out over the crowds below. I felt privileged to sit next to Miss Shaw, the

Chinese students, their parents, and Miss Wang, but through it all, Madam Hung Chin weighed heavily on my mind.

"Look, the famous Mrs. Arlington is here," Miss Shaw said, discreetly pointing to the front row's reserved seats below us. We craned our necks to see and, almost as if sensing our curiosity, Mrs. Arlington turned around. Her English face was an unnatural flush of pink from too much powder, and her thin lips a garish red. Even from our distance, there was no hiding her wrinkles. If only Madam could have seen this, I thought to myself, hardly able to concentrate, though I clapped and laughed on cue, as I looked to Miss Shaw for guidance.

"Is everything alright?" Miss Shaw asked, leaning against me at intermission. I can still remember the fragrant scent of her lilac perfume, and the way her freckled hands lay in her lap as her fingers twitched slightly with her concern.

"Everything alright," I mumbled, and was relieved when Trevor, who was next to me, passed me an Icy Mint and I sucked on it in silence.

The afternoon seemed particularly bright when we emerged from the theatre. The sun was warm on my skin and my hair sticky from sweat. I thanked Miss Shaw as the group split up and we went our separate ways. I walked alone, buoyed only by the prospect of sharing my recent pleasure with Madam.

When I got to Luke Lane, I noticed that the shop was closed. Perhaps Madam was still not well. I let myself in through the back entrance. I found her black-encrusted kettle, lukewarm in a sea of powdery ashes on the coal stove.

"Madam!" I called out sharply, but there was no reply. My heart pounded, I walked a few feet to her bedroom, and parted the curtain of beads in the doorway. Madam was lying across the bed, and the thin sheet she usually used as her cover had slipped to the floor. She must be asleep, I thought, for I had seen her like that before, with her long hair spilled across the pillow and her lips curved into a smile.

"Sweet dreams, Madam," I said softly. Then I saw that her teacup was on the floor at the foot of the bed. I went to pick it up, and found that the tea was untouched and had gone cold. Even before I touched her, I knew that she was gone.

The profound shock of Madam's death cannot be expressed in words. Nothing could staunch my tears or fill the void and stop the sudden surge of loneliness. The person I loved more than any other was gone out of my reach. I felt the weight of the world and its concerns as I grieved.

"Madam Hung Chin ... Madam Hung Chin," I sobbed as I buried my face in her soft sheets, overcome with rage at being abandoned.

It was already dark outside before I could bring myself to leave her. I tentatively covered her with her pale cotton sheet, and set right the few things she kept beside her bed on an upturned crate—her tortoiseshell comb, her hairbrush, her night water glass, and the set of ivory dominos that had been her husband's, which she kept beside her small black bible, inside of which was an old photograph. It was perhaps the only photograph of herself that she ever allowed to be taken. She was young then and slim in that frayed sepia shot, and her hair was a cascade of black silk.

"I won't forget you," I said as I tucked the photograph into my shirt pocket, the shirt she had starched and ironed so carefully for my outing to the theatre. Then I quickly unclasped her gold heart chain, which was her pride, and put it around my neck before reluctantly turning away to retrieve the red book with the Hakka legend of Hung Lin.

I didn't know where I was going when I stepped out into the moonlight in our backyard, but I wanted to stay out of sight and not attract attention. I hopped the fence between the properties, and ran through the eerie shadows of the garment factories, too frightened to notice the transients who frequented those haunts at night, and too scared to remain alone in Madam's house of death. I remembered stories my mother told me about sleeping in shelters and marketplaces, and felt that I was not as brave as she was and besides, I couldn't stop my feet from running. It seemed as though I ran all night until I found myself on South Camp Road, not far from the Chinese school. I stood in front of the school building, heart thumping and exhausted. Then, as if Madam herself prompted me, I raced up the dark walkway, past the sleepy rose garden and the alamander bush, feeling light-headed in the rarefied air. I paused on the veranda to catch my breath, unable to suppress fresh tears before I banged on Miss Shaw's door. When she didn't answer, I pounded harder until my fists hurt. I leaned against her door in frustration until I felt the door give way as it opened slightly. Through the narrow opening I saw Miss Shaw in her housecoat, her red ringlets dishevelled. She had been sleeping. Her blue eyes registered surprise as she recognized me. She bent down, wrapped her slim arms around me, and ushered me in from the night.

"What's the matter, dear one?" she said, her voice trembling with compassion. I sobbed afresh and told her everything as she held me in her arms, listening.

"I'll take care of things," she said. "Don't you worry, pet. I'll take care of it all."

I was too young to understand the arrangements that funerals involved, too young to be expected to keep the shop going, and too young to know the intricacies of Madam's mortgage and important documents. All I remember is that Miss Shaw fetched the rest of my clothes from the house and, at my request, the vic-trola, and it was she who stood by my side as Madam was buried, after a moving eulogy at the Half Way Tree Parish Church, in the adjoining cemetery.

"You'll have to stay with me, John, until proper arrangements are made," she said. "It's not that I don't want you, you must understand that, but everything must be done legally and above board."

* * * * *

The living room with the colourful rugs, photographs, and vases of fresh-cut roses was where I spent most of my time while at Miss Shaw's. I brooded in the lonely silence of its dim interior. Drifting in and out of my own worlds, I constantly watched specks of dust, rays of light, and passing shadows. In the evenings, by lamplight, I curled into a ball on the sofa, half expecting to see Madam in her pale cotton shift, and I listened for her familiar voice. There were times in my imaginings when, from the corners of my eyes, I thought I saw steam rise from a phantom teacup in the dark, and I would turn around quickly to see her, but she was always elusive, beyond the edge of sunbeams or the sooty darkness and the lonely melody of the house as it sighed and shifted in the night, brick against board against stone.

"I'm going to teach you proper English," Miss Shaw said one Sunday morning, coming into the living room with a copy of an American newspaper. "Speaking too much Hakka has ruined your grammar, and if you are to get anywhere in life, you must have a good command of English."

Furious, I broke my silence.

"You can't take Madam away!" I screamed through tears as I pounded my fists into the soft velvet cushion. "Don't even try!"

"Honey, I can never do that. You ought to know that. All I want is to teach you to read the newspaper. It will open up the world for you and help with your language, too. Remember, I told you I'm American. If you knew the things written in these papers, you'd know all about the foolishness that is going on in America—shootings of innocent people, lynching of Negroes. Lots of things happening at home make me both mad and scared. And Chicago where I'm from is no better. Ever heard of Al Capone?"

"No, who's he?"

"He's just about the worst mobster that ever walked the earth, and now he's taken over Chicago! He controls everything, John, including the police! It is no wonder my father had the foresight to send me here to Jamaica. Yes, John, this house and property belongs to us. My dad must have known that I'd enjoy the independence, not to mention the experience of working as a storyteller."

"Is you father still in Chicago?"

"Yes, honey, and to make matters worse, he's not well. He hasn't been the same since he fought in the war—chills, fevers, and headaches, that sort of thing. And he certainly is not up for travelling."

Miss Shaw came over to the sofa where I sat lost in thought, trying to picture the mobster Al Capone in faraway America. She silently opened the newspaper and pointed to one of the articles.

"Read this," she said. "Look what's happening."

I leaned closer and read aloud about a dark-skinned American singer and dancer named Josephine Baker, who had left America in discontent to live in France.

"John, many Americans are treated like second-class citizens," Miss Shaw said pensively. "They are despised because of the colour of their skin. Some are as poor as the folk I've seen begging here. No, America is no heaven, and there is even a despicable organization called the Ku Klux Klan that nurtures racial hatred. That kind of hate is called prejudice. It's a terrible thing, John, and I really hope you'll never be exposed to it. Remember when I first met you and I couldn't take my eyes off of you? Well, it was because you reminded me of a little boy I once loved. He was my brother Rory's son, Eugene. He had the same wonderful colouring as you—fair hair, light eyes and skin. His mother, Anne, was a Negro from the southern states, whom my brother met while teaching in Georgia. Everyone warned them, even I did, but love wouldn't let them listen. They went ahead and got married, though they received several anonymous death threats in the mail, and when Eugene was only three, someone made good on those threats. My brother and his family were murdered in their Alabama home on a hot summer night. It was a terrible tragedy, John, a very terrible tragedy."

* * * * *

Newspapers came regularly from America, and it seemed that every Sunday, Miss Shaw and I pondered over and discussed world affairs.

"Your English is getting better," she said one morning. "And you are more aware of the world out there. I have been thinking of sending you to a new school—Kingston College, perhaps. Madam had paid your fees here for another two years and the time is drawing to a close already. In fact, Miss Wang and I have been talking about things and she agrees."

I was too stunned to respond. I turned away from her and the newspaper, mumbling.

"Speak up, honey," she said, leaning closer.

"I don't want to go."

"Why?"

"Don't know."

I wrung my hands in desperation, unable to come up with a reason, knowing full well that it was because the Chinese school and speaking Hakka were my last links to Madam.

CHAPTER 5

Telling Tales

*B*ecause of Miss Shaw's position as a foreign storyteller, she was invited into homes that the average Jamaican, or the poorer classes such as myself, would not have had access to. But once in a while, she would coax me into going along with her, and she would assume a playfulness I rarely saw in grownups.

"Pretend you are my nephew," she'd whisper as we sat together at dinner tables. Plates of rice and peas, plantains, roast chicken, and potato salad were passed around, and she would nudge me under the table, egging me on to share exchanges with her about world affairs.

"Well, John, my young nephew," she would say formally. "How about that sled dog in America called Balto? What a hero, eh, John?" Her words would draw everyone's attention to her.

"Tell the good people here about him," she said with merriment, fully aware that all eyes were turning from her to my blond, light-eyed self. No doubt when I replied with a well-practised American accent, all present thought I was American.

"Yes, Aunt Fiona," I replied with relish. "That poor dog ran 650 miles through ice and snow."

"Why?" asked a swarthy woman with coarse black hair and a green satin hat, her fork suspended halfway between her plate and her lips. "Why would any dog run all that distance?"

I immediately launched into explanations I had read in the foreign newspapers, and the upper-class locals nodded their heads in admiration.

"People were sick with diphtheria in Alaska," I said, revelling in the looks of interest at the table. "So Balto, the dog, led a team that delivered medicine all the way up north through the blinding snow."

"Amazing!" said a church minister, and I wasn't sure if he meant my knowledge or the dog's achievement.

"Astounding at least," Miss Shaw retorted, "considering Alaska is so isolated and cold."

Ours was the sort of conversation that turned heads at gatherings, and we both attended many. They were usually held in the church minister's home on Constant Spring Road, where Miss Shaw, dressed in silks, would tell Ojibwa tales and then, dressed in linen, at the doctor's residence on Duke Street, where she outdid herself telling tales from the southern United States about slavery. At the school headmaster's house on Old Hope Road, she brought to life the tales of loggers working in the American forests.

Miss Shaw, the consummate performer, who must have been no more than twenty-five years old, became more mischievous with each social event. Together we laughed hysterically about my fake accent, and she praised me for having an ear for language and pronunciation. She was extremely fond of the theatrics, of passing me off as her son, her brother, or any other family member that suited her playfulness, though she meant no harm with her deceptions.

* * * * *

In spite of those intimate times together, Miss Shaw went ahead with making arrangements to enrol me in Kingston College, which ultimately meant that we would spend less time together and result in my acquiring an identity that would no longer fit in with her world of play-acting. I contemplated that future with trepidation, and spent as much of what little time I had left with the Chinese students. Even Miss Wang's incessant hammering on the piano was comforting.

"Want to play marbles?" I'd ask the Chinese boys hopefully, and before long we all would be engaged for hours in games of war, with toy soldiers on the concrete walkway. There were times when both the boys and girls enjoyed the same games, such as when we played hopscotch and "I Come to See Janey," in which the ghost of a dead girl would chase all the participants. How deliciously scared I was playing that game. Those were wonderful days of camaraderie, though inevitably my childhood began slipping away.

Late one evening, after the students and Miss Wang had left for home, Miss Shaw and I were sitting on the front veranda. The sun was slowly dying, and the scent of roses perfumed the air. Small green lizards that were active during the daytime were clinging to branches, settling down for the night.

Miss Shaw was engrossed in a book of folktales. I was on the tiled floor nearby, absorbed with a colony of small black ants that had come up from between the tiles. I watched the ants scurry. Then I dropped a piece of soda cracker into their path and watched with delight as they hauled huge chunks of the cracker back into their hole. I was about to call Miss Shaw's attention to them when the ringing of a bicycle bell startled us both.

The rider was in the blue trousers and white shirt uniform of the Jamaican Postal Service, and his expression looked both official and officious.

"I is looking for Miss Shaw," he said, pulling a paper from his breast pocket, next to a sweaty armpit.

Miss Shaw stood up nervously and put her book aside before going down the broad steps.

"I'm Miss Shaw."

"Sign this paper, ma'am," the man said gruffly.

I saw her pale hand scrawl her signature as she smiled, then reached into her skirts and gave him a tip.

He stood by and watched as Miss Shaw silently read the telegram.

"Is bad news, ma'am?" the rider asked, unable to contain his curiosity.

"Yes, my father has taken seriously ill, and I have to return to America as soon as possible because it is believed that he is dying."

*****

"I have an appointment with the King's representative," Miss Shaw said lamely the day after getting the telegram. "I want to adopt you, John, but I don't know what to do about taking you to America. There will be lots of red tape to get through, and time is short."

"What will happen to me then?"

"I don't know because although you might look Caucasian, we both know that you are not, and with racial tensions so high back home, I would have to give consent to someone here to look after you until my return."

"Could I stay in this house?"

"No, John, I'm closing the house. Only the school will be open."

The same conversation came up again and again. I felt helplessly alone and distraught, and was sitting on the sofa sulking when someone came to the door, knocking timidly. Miss Shaw opened it to find an elderly Chinese man, dressed in his Sunday suit. The old man peered into the room and on seeing me, brushed past Miss Shaw.

"Ah," he said, sounding relieved. "You the one who speak Hakka, yes?"

"Here, have a seat." Miss Shaw said, pointing out a chair. But the old man came over to the sofa where I sat. "I'm Ming Wong," he said, then proceeded to speak in Hakka. "You must be John Moneague. I am Madam Hung Chin's lawyer. I have been looking at her file, but she sent the original copies of all her important documents to China, with her late husband, so I am powerless. Her shop on Luke Lane has been closed and will be taken over by the city if there is no word from other lawyers in China. Her possessions will also be impounded until then. It is believed she was in contact with a law firm in Bejing, but no one knows for sure. Have you heard from this law firm?"

"No."

"Well, stay in touch, and if you hear anything at all, contact me, okay? Here is my address, John."

I folded the piece of paper with Mr. Wong's Orange Street address on it, and explained to Miss Shaw about the purpose of his visit.

* * * * *

The next afternoon Miss Shaw hired a car, and we arrived at the Lady Musgrave Road address of the King's representative. We walked up the palm tree-lined walkway, wearing our finest clothes, and admired the sunken garden to the left of the residence. Never had I seen such a burst of colour, for zinnias were in bloom, as well as hibiscus and lilies and orchids. An English butler met us at the door and informed us that it was not possible to see the representative, since his time was taken up with appeasing possible uprisings on sugar estates in the countryside, where disgruntled workers were demanding more pay.

"But I have to leave the country," Miss Shaw pleaded. "It is urgent that I see him. Is he not here?"

"No, madam," the butler replied haughtily. "He has been

recommending that people like yourself see Mrs. Arlington, for she is free to handle trivial matters."

"This is not a trivial matter," said Miss Shaw, arching her brow.

"Well, now it is," the arrogant butler said as he quickly closed the door in our faces.

* * * * *

An hour later, Miss Shaw and I were taken by hired car to the home of Mrs. Arlington. The driver, a smiling East Indian man with broken teeth, was eager to regale us with local gossip. Hearing that we were intent on visiting Arlington House, he told us with relish that Mrs. Arlington had taken over her husband's prestigious position in the government as assistant to the King's representative because her husband had taken up with a much younger English woman, who had come to the island to help out in his office. As it turned out, he left his wife of twenty-five years and returned to England with his mistress.

"How sad," Miss Shaw said, feeling genuine sympathy.

"Not sad for that young gal, though, 'cause them say him'a breed her, and she going get a ton'a money."

I watched in silence as Miss Shaw covered her mouth with her long fingers and turned her head away, and I wasn't sure if she was concealing a smile or a sigh.

We didn't have long to wait on the spacious veranda of Arlington House. Shortly after we knocked, the door was opened by a black-skinned servant girl of about sixteen, wearing the traditional white cap and apron of servants on the island.

"Is Mrs. Arlington in?" Miss Shaw inquired, trying her best to peer past the girl into the house.

"Who should I say is asking?" said the girl in a well-practised clipped tone.

"Tell her it is Fiona Shaw, the American storyteller."

The girl closed the door gently, then returned almost

immediately to usher us into the elegant hall. Our steps echoed noisily, and I couldn't help but wonder if we left a dirt trail as we walked. From an archway I saw the drawing-room, which looked like a room in Buckingham Palace, for there were portraits on the walls, Persian rugs on the floor, sofas, padded chairs, chests, and all manner of antique mahogany furnishings. In a corner there was a small theatre, about three feet by four feet, complete with red velvet curtains and satin drawstrings, and, to my delight, a variety of hand puppets hanging from a bracket on the wall close by. My interest was piqued. However, it was at that precise moment that Mrs. Arlington entered the room. She looked paler than I had expected and her hair was whiter, and there were brown age spots on her neck and hands. She was impeccably dressed in a blue linen sundress.

"Good afternoon," she said, a painted smile on her lips. "What brings you here, Miss Shaw?"

Miss Shaw gripped my hand, and I could almost hear her swallow before she spoke.

"It is a long story, Mrs. Arlington, but I'll make it short. I have to return to the States tonight on an urgent family matter. I also want to adopt John, the boy here with me, but there will be reams of red tape to get through, and I don't have a lot of time, so I would have to let him remain here in Jamaica until my return."

Mrs. Arlington stretched her wrinkled neck and looked down her nose at me.

"Is the boy not an American then?" she asked haughtily.

"No."

"Well, is he a British subject? I am only authorized to serve his Majesty's subjects."

"Yes, yes, he is a British subject."

"Splendid, Miss Shaw, let's continue this discussion in my office. The boy would best remain here in the drawing room. He might entertain himself with ... let's see ... ah, how about the puppet theatre? It was a wretched gift from a European ambassador. What use would I have for such a thing!"

* * * * *

Left alone with the puppet theatre, I explored it inside and out. I ran my fingers along the red velvet curtains, marvelling at its beauty. I felt the smoothness of its sturdy wood-panelled frame, and was pleasantly surprised to find that it was collapsible. I eagerly unhooked the puppets from the wall and admired their exquisite details. They were carved in lightweight wood and painted with expressive features. There were wolves, pigs, princes, princesses, and peasants, and even a Japanese geisha girl.

At first, I tried performing Red Riding Hood, changing voices with each character. Then, growing bolder, I began to create my own skits, using various accents and puppets, and I even had the Japanese puppet speaking in Hakka, which amused me greatly and I couldn't help but laugh out loud.

When my performance was over, I was surprised to hear enthusiastic applause. I stepped out from behind the theatre to find Miss Shaw and Mrs. Arlington sitting across the room.

Mrs. Arlington immediately rose and came toward me.

"What a splendid imagination you have, John, and what a variety of voices! You are a very talented boy. Miss Shaw and I have been discussing your situation, and I want to let you know that I have come to a decision. You will be pleased to know that while Miss Shaw is away in America, you will be able to stay here in Kingston with a British family who live on Duke Street. They are Dr. and Mrs. Meitner."

CHAPTER 6

The Meitners

Miss Shaw's ship, the *Annie Sutton*, left Kingston Harbour for New York later that evening. Our parting was a hurried one, though she assured me that her trip would be short. The hardest part, she said, would be waiting for the connections between New York and Chicago. I stood dry-eyed on the dock waving, though I doubt that she could have seen me below, among the crowd gathered there. Some were curiosity seekers, while others were there to see friends and relatives off. Miss Shaw stood on the upper deck, looking pale, and her red curls, though pinned up, were already flying in the wind. I watched until my legs ached from standing, even as the ship slowly moved away from the shore. I watched it part the choppy sea. White foam clung to its prow, and then it disappeared in the distance. And I heard the call of a night bird and felt overwhelmed with loneliness. Miss Shaw had been my closest companion for the last two years.

"See you soon," I whispered into the evening air, tears stinging my eyes as I turned on my heel. Miss Wang was waiting for me in a horse-drawn buggy. She had also come to say goodbye, and a suitcase with my belongings was sitting alongside her. "Well, John," she said in Hakka, "she gone. She was a very dear friend. I only hope she come back 'cause I hear so much about America that not good, and to imagine that is Chicago she have to go to, and it so full of crime there. But don't worry you head, John. I know you going miss her, but look at it like this. Tonight is the start of a new chapter in your life, and if it turn out that you don't like this doctor they sending you to, there is always Miss Shaw coming back for you, okay?"

"Yes, Miss Wang."

"Let's go then, 'cause now that car and buggy side by side on the Kingston roads, the horse them get frighten when them hear car horn, and my horse nervous already."

＊＊＊＊＊

It was very dark when the horse clip-clopped along Duke Street. The offices and residential buildings were well kept and upper class. There were no stray goats or dogs wandering about. There was only the sound of crickets and the low rumble of distant thunder.

"It might rain," said Miss Wang, straining to see the house numbers. Then she slowed the buggy to a crawl, and I noticed the scent of the sea in the air. I thought of Miss Shaw. We approached a two-storey building with a dark hedge in front and an iron gate leading to a stone walkway. Straining my eyes in the fading light, I made out the number 24.

"We are here," Miss Wang said solemnly. "But it going rain, so I'll take you to the door, but won't stay long 'cause I don't want to get caught in a storm. The horse would go mad. You'll be alright, John. May God be with you."

"Thanks, Miss Wang." I didn't know what else to say as I gulped back tears, for the evening's emotions had already taken their toll. "Tell the school children I'll come to visit."

The gate was already open. Together we walked up to the house, both of us holding onto my bulky suitcase. By the time we made it up to the veranda, lightning split the sky. Miss Wang dropped the suitcase on the tiles, hurried to the door, then knocked loudly.

A maid, dressed in uniform, answered.

"Good evening, ma'am," she said, her brown eyes looking merry.

"Good evening," Miss Wang said. "We're here to see the Meitners. I think they expecting this boy here, John Moneague."

"Yes, yes, them expecting him, but them had was to go out 'cause of a emergency. But I'll look after Master John till them get back. My name is Clarissa, Master John. And if you haven't tasted my beef soup yet, you haven't tasted anything. Come sit at the table. You must be so hungry, right? Them did set a spot for you already."

The moment I walked across the carpeted floor, Miss Wang turned away, perhaps so that I wouldn't see her tears. Then when she briefly looked over her shoulder, her long black hair hid her eyes.

"Good luck," she said, quickly excusing herself as she departed.

I was alone. Clarissa had gone to the kitchen, and from there I could hear her talking and laughing, and it took me a while to realize that she was talking to me. She returned to the dining room, carrying a tray with a small white bowl of soup, two slices of bread, and small dish with a pat of butter.

"Enjoy," she said with a broad smile. "And if you want seconds, I have more in the kitchen. I is hoping you going like staying here. The doctor is a good man, him been kind to me and my boy, so I just know that him going be good to you too."

"Thanks," I said, bending over the soup. I looked up and saw that Clarissa looked alarmed, her brown eyes incredulous.

"Stop!" she said. "You not going say you grace!! We have to remember to say prayers here, even if silent. We mustn't forget we is Christian, 'cause the doctor and him wife is Jews. Is you a Jew? If you is, I'm sorry. But we Christian mustn't lose sight of who we is."

"No, I'm not Jewish, I'm Christian, but I don't know how to pray."

Clarissa rolled her eyes in disbelief.

"Well, let me teach you. We better be quick before them come back. Just do what I do. Put you hands them together in you lap. Shut you eyes, then talk to God quiet, and say: 'We give thee thanks, Almighty God, for which we are about to receive, from thy bounty through Christ Our Lord. Amen.' It quick, but God will hear. Now go on, eat."

I was on my second bowl when the front door rattled. Clarissa took a lamp from a side table and went through the dining room, the living room, and on into the front hall. I heard a male voice with a strong English accent, a woman's gentle murmur, and Clarissa's sympathetic baritone. I couldn't make out words. I put my spoon aside, patted my napkin on my lips, ran a hand through my thick hair, and, with my legs rigid under the table, waited.

Clarissa, carrying the lamp, re-entered the dining room, followed by Dr. Meitner. He looked pale, middle-aged, and weary, with sad hazel eyes and black brows that were almost as thick as his moustache. He was wearing a dark, nondescript suit that blended in with the house's dim interior, but when he saw me sitting there, a sad solitary figure at the table, he broke into a warm smile and came toward me.

"John Moneague," he said with gusto. "What a pleasure it is to meet you. Mrs. Arlington told us to expect you tonight, but we were called away urgently, so I must apologize. There was a fire on Barry Street. Three buildings were destroyed, but fortunately, no loss of life. Stand up, young man. Let's have a look at you."

I stood up nervously, holding onto the arm of my chair for support, just as Mrs. Meitner came into the room. She looked younger than I had expected, though her sharp eyes betrayed worldliness. She wore her dark hair pinned up, as many foreigners did. With her blue eyes and smooth olive complexion, she was beautiful.

"Pleased to meet you, John," she said, and I found that her grip was firm and confident.

"So how was the soup?" she asked. "Clarissa is certainly the best cook we have ever had. I wouldn't want to lose her. Don't you agree, Edvard?"

"Yes, Sarah, you're right. I've become so accustomed to her looking after us, I don't know what we'd do without her."

Clarissa smiled shyly throughout the exchange, but then I found that all eyes were on me awaiting my opinion.

"The soup was excellent," I said, meaning it. "I had two bowls."

Mrs. Meitner smiled. "You're going to become one of her biggest fans," she said teasingly.

"Well, she will have to teach me how to cook like that, so that when I go back to Miss Shaw's, I won't miss it too much."

* * * * *

I was given a room on the second floor overlooking the street. What a great pleasure it was to watch the world below from my window. I watched when a ragged black-skinned man, selling brooms, came to the gate and was paid a few coins for two brooms, and I watched as another man, this one an albino, arrived on a bicycle selling fish. He showed the contents of a deep straw basket full of fish to Clarissa, and I knew from the way he balanced the weighty basket on the dripping bicycle that it also contained pieces of swiftly melting ice wrapped in cloth and saw-dust to help to keep the fish fresh.

It was like being in a theatre in which people came and went constantly like actors. Mango, pineapple, and coconut vendors stopped by, and an old coolie woman, pretending to be blind, sold flowers along the street. I had seen her a few buildings up from ours, walking normally, then as she approached our house, she would pretend to stumble and feel her way along the hedge, calling out, "Fresh flowers, buy fresh flowers!" Mrs. Meitner once told me that the only thing fresh about those flowers was that they were freshly robbed from graves.

Then there were Dr. Meitner's patients who came regularly to his small practice on the ground floor. I found them interesting enough to create stories about them, in much the same manner as Miss Shaw would have done. Many of his patients were the well-off British, as well as Syrians and Jews. I cannot remember ever seeing any Coloureds.

There were times when I sat alone in my room at that window, wondering about my life and why it was that after two years with Miss Shaw, she had not adopted me. Did she think she was protecting me by not making things legal? I wondered what Madam Hung Chin would have thought about my new life, and if somehow my mother knew what had become of me. Every once in a while when I looked into the mirror on my bureau and saw my light-skinned face and my grey eyes, I wondered if I looked like my father, whom everyone had said was a sailor.

Every evening at six, Dr. Meitner would come out of his downstairs office and into the dining room. He would ring a small bell to summon the rest of the household, and then we would sit down to enjoy the evening meal, never forgetting to compliment Clarissa on her culinary skills. One night, after I had been with them for a week, I asked the Meitners' permission to watch Clarissa at work in the kitchen.

"How extraordinary!" Dr. Meitner exclaimed. "I would never have thought of you as a cook."

"I used to cook Hakka dishes when I lived with Madam," I blurted out, licking my lips at the memory.

"What are Hakka dishes?" Mrs. Meitner asked, looking somewhat bemused, putting aside her napkin and dessert spoon.

"It's Chinese. The Hakkas are a proud ethnic group from China."

"And where did you learn all this, young man?" said Dr. Meitner, his eyes lighting up with interest as he pushed his plate aside.

"Madam Hung Chin taught me everything, and besides, I went to a Chinese school."

"Extraordinary!" Dr. Meitner said, quickly cleaning his fingers in the finger bowl. "I'd never have taken you for Chinese!"

We laughed, but although I knew they were curious about my origins, I kept the information to myself.

"You can certainly watch Clarissa in the kitchen," said Mrs. Meitner. "I know she would love the company, but it sounds to me as though you two could exchange recipes."

"Do you know how to play chess?" Dr. Meitner interjected. "Chess is like the game of life. You have to learn to be always a step ahead of your opponent. You mustn't show weakness, you have to let your opponent believe that you are skilled. I'm sure you know what I mean, John."

"I've never played," I replied hesitantly.

"Then I will have to teach you, but I have a feeling you will have no difficulty learning because you already know how to stay ahead of the enemy."

I didn't know why it was, but I couldn't warm to the Meitners, not in those first few days anyway. I watched their comings and goings with trepidation and some amount of suspicion, thinking that something did not sit right, but couldn't put my finger on it.

* * * * *

"What you cooking, Clarissa?"

"Stew peas, but I not g'wane put no pig's tail in it 'cause the Meitners, them is Jews and don't eat pork. But since it hard to get ingredient these days, it just as well 'cause since wartime, me had was to come up with different ways to make things. Everything scarce now."

"What you going put in it then?"

"Salt beef. The sailor them bring salt beef. Bless them. Me buy piece, and me was able to get a big gill of red peas, and it last long, you see, and the other day the coconut man manage to find a dry one for me. And since we always have thyme and escallion handy, we in business."

"It going take long to make it, Clarissa?"

"Not too long, Master John. Me soak the peas and the salt beef already."

"How long it take to cook?"

"Maybe an hour or two."

"What you going do with that flour in the bowl, Clarissa?"

"Oh that, I going make spinners, a kind of dumpling, but flour is scarce, so me can't use nuff."

"How you going put in that piece of coconut?"

"I g'wane grate the white part and soak it in water till milk form."

"What a lot of things you have to do to make stew peas."

Clarissa smiled. "In life we have to do lots of things slowly and carefully. It is the way of the Lord."

While we were waiting for the stew peas to cook, I occupied myself by playing with a small pile of sun-bleached assorted seashells that I had found on the windowsill and, tiring of them, I gazed out absently at the lush backyard with its fruit-laden mango trees and noticed the half-hidden side entrance to Dr. Meitner's practice. I instinctively knew that it was out of bounds, and felt a certain inquisitive thrill. Clarissa went into the dining room to set the table, and I watched a fair-skinned gentleman, with his head kept well down, make his way through the back-yard to knock softly on Dr. Meitner's office door. His presence aroused my interest, for in spite of the heat, he was impeccably dressed in a suit and tie. However, he emerged from the doctor's office almost immediately in the company of an elegantly dressed blonde woman, wearing a black hat, her face totally obscured by a veil. A few minutes later, a dark-haired man, dressed in a crumpled beige suit, arrived. He reminded me of the gangsters I had seen in the American newspapers, and I imagined him to be Al Capone and hoped that he wouldn't see me at the window. I also

57

imagined that Dr. Meitner, who in reality might have been kind and sensitive, was, in my mind, performing horrific amputations and brain transplants in his office. I kept my eyes trained on his door, half expecting to see blood oozing out from under the doorway. But what I saw was "Al Capone," looking perfectly normal when he came out, carrying a brown paper bag. He stood below the mango trees, circled them, then stopped to pick a few of the ripest fruit before going on his way. Then, quite unexpectedly, a young black-skinned boy, about my age, burst around the corner of the yard, pushing an old metal cartwheel. He came right up to the kitchen window, and was startled to find me there. We stared at each other a full five minutes before either of us said anything.

"Who're you?" I finally asked, knowing he was not one of the doctor's patients.

"I is Gerald," he said slowly, a piece of grass dangling from his lip. "Clarissa is me mother."

"Oh," I said, "she mentioned you. I'm John."

Clarissa heard voices, and hurried into the kitchen. She came over to where I stood at the window and leaned out, her bulk squeezing against me. I saw Gerald duck down behind the fragrant rose bushes, his eyes full of mischief.

"I know is you that Gerald," Clarissa said gruffly, concealing her pleasure. "Just you leave dat piece of rusty iron contraption out there before you come inside. I don't want no mess in here. And take that grass out'a you mouth. You can't talk to people like that. Show respect. Master John is here in'a the kitchen. Is time you meet him."

Gerald leaned the rusty wheel against the side of the house, then wiped his hands on the back of his trousers before coming inside. "Wipe you feet," Clarissa ordered, pointing to the thick straw mat at the door, and it was then that I realized that Gerald's feet were bare.

"You can carry one of the stool them over to the small table in'a the corner, Gerald," Clarissa said. "I make stew peas, and I know is your favourite. You can have some now 'cause the Meitner, them going have them own later."

Gerald hurriedly dragged a stool over to a paint-chipped table in the farthest corner of the kitchen, which was partially hidden by the stand Clarissa used for hanging up her cooking utensils.

"Master John," she said with a grin, "this monkey here is me son Gerald."

"Hello," I said, my eyes drawn to Gerald's calloused feet, his shabby clothes, his warm smile, and the crude way he held his spoon. "I think we just met," I said.

Gerald smiled self-consciously, showing perfect white teeth, and I noticed that his cropped kinky hair was as dark as my Chinese friends', and his bright eyes as brown, although his skin, unlike theirs, was as dark as polished leather.

"How old are you?" I asked, unsure of what else to say. At first, Gerald did not speak as he tried unsuccessfully to make himself smaller at the table, perhaps hoping that I would go away.

"Me is twelve," he finally answered, hanging his head as though waiting for an execution.

"So am I," I said, feeling somewhat awkward with his silence. Then it dawned on me that Gerald knew nothing of my past. How was he to know that I, too, was from a poor background, and that I, too, though I did not look it, was Coloured?

"Do you live near here?" I asked hopefully.

Gerald shook his head and mumbled. "Gerald, speak up," Clarissa called over to him. "When Master John talk to you, you must answer. And another thing, call him Master John. Is for respect, you hear?"

* * * * *

One afternoon, three weeks after I went to stay at the Meitners', a chauffeur-driven car arrived at our gate. The chauffeur was in uniform, which signified that he was on official business. Clarissa went down the walkway to investigate why he was honking his horn in such an excited manner. I saw them from my window, speaking rapidly. Then Clarissa turned and walked back toward the house. I watched the chauffeur get out and unload a large cardboard box from the trunk before following Clarissa up the walkway. I was still watching from the window when I heard a knock at my door.

"Master John, is me Clarissa. I have a note for you from a Mrs. Arlington."

She handed me the note and watched as I tore open the envelope. "Dear John Moneague," the note said. "I have had word from your guardian, Miss Shaw. She will be delayed in Chicago. Her father has taken a turn for the worse. I know the Meitners are looking after you well and will continue to do so. I am sending a gift for you to amuse yourself with in the meantime. In His Majesty's service, Mrs. Arlington."

Clarissa and I looked at each other, each feeling the other's excitement.

"I wonder what the good Lord send for you now," Clarissa said, her eyes shining with anticipation as together we flew down the steps, two at a time, to meet the chauffeur on the veranda. He was standing, cap in hand, fanning himself from the heat, and had carefully leaned the box on its side. I felt as though I hardly dared open it, but, encouraged by Clarissa, I quickly broke the strings and lifted a flap.

Inside was the collapsible puppet theatre, as well as a straw bag stuffed with all the puppets, and I was more than amazed at my good fortune!

"Please thank Mrs. Arlington for me," I said to the chauffeur. My voice was hoarse with excitement, though when I thought about Miss Shaw's delay in Chicago, my heart grew heavy with regret.

CHAPTER 7

Portland

*T*he puppet stage was set up in the drawing-room that evening. Two tall, bright kerosene lamps were placed nearby on tables, and the room was bathed in their golden glow. Even Mrs. Meitner, who usually worked in her room, came to join the audience. It was an evening of laughter and pleasant memories, mostly because the Meitners seemed less formal, as did Clarissa and Gerald, who watched from the doorway, conscious of the unwritten code that barred them from being allowed in the drawing room as guests.

When the performance was over, I glanced out the front windows. It was pitch-black outside, for the street lamps were not lit, perhaps due to shortages, and the darkness gave the impression that the city was folded in a dark velvet fabric. I felt weary and said goodnight, then took one of the lamps, which was already attracting an assortment of night insects, and started up the staircase to my bedroom. On the way up, a movement below attracted my attention, and from where I stood, I saw the Meitners quickly retire to an adjoining downstairs room, which they often referred to as the library. I watched in silence as they drew a pair of chairs up to a mahogany table, their heads together conspiratorially. Something of their unusual closeness held my attention.

When Dr. Meitner moved even closer to his wife, I wasn't sure of his intent, but then I saw him gently cup and caress her full breasts as he leaned toward her. I should have continued on my way, but could not for fear of the stairs squeaking and alerting them to my presence. They did not see me as they stood up slowly and held one another urgently, their expressions luminous with ecstasy. My body ached from wanting escape. I turned my head away, but could not erase the image, and as the lamplight flickered, I looked and saw the doctor's hand slide under the folds of his wife's voluminous skirts, revealing her shapely thigh, which was as white as alabaster.

There was such a knot in my gut, I could barely stand, and it was not until I heard Clarissa's footsteps on the wooden floor as she approached from the kitchen, carrying a tray with their nightcap, that they reluctantly pulled apart, and pretended to examine atlases and what appeared to be hand-drawn maps.

I was too wound up to sleep and felt a need to talk with someone. I took the opportunity to sneak back down the stairs, past the library, to the kitchen, knowing that Gerald would still be there. I saw him sitting at the servants' table saying his grace, and I was humbled. He saw me come in. He smiled shyly and wiped the corners of his mouth with the back of his hand, for he had been eating a slice of bread, which he put back onto his enamel plate on my approach.

"Hello, Gerald," I said, taking a stool over to the table.

"Hello, Master John," he mumbled. "T'was a good show."

"Thanks. Is it alright if I sit here?" I asked, noticing how skittish he had become, watching the doorway.

"Master John," Clarissa said sternly, coming back into the kitchen with her tray. "You can't sit there. The Meitners might think we getting too even, and the Lord knows that is not my intention."

"Sorry," I said, bewildered by the rules of etiquette. "I just wanted to talk to Gerald."

"That okay, but you mustn't sit with him, you hear?"

I barely had time to say two words to Gerald before Mrs.

Meitner herself came into the kitchen, looking pensive yet expressing no surprise at finding me there, and I wondered if she suspected that I had witnessed the recent activities in the library.

"It's getting late, Clarissa," she said, avoiding my eyes. "It's time to shut down the kitchen and bolt the doors. We have a lot to do in the morning, as discussed before."

I searched her face, but there were no signs of embarrassment. It was only I who felt awkward and self-conscious about what I saw.

* * * * *

June 26, 1927, is a date I will never forget. I was awakened in the early hours of the morning by loud noises. Then I heard murmurs, whispers, and strange low voices in the dark. I sat up in bed, too terrified to move any further. A darting light outside attracted my attention. I craned my neck to see what it was, but because it was so dark, I found it impossible to see anything. I slipped out of bed cautiously, convinced that the house was being burgled, and was about to open my bedroom door a crack when Mrs. Meitner came into my room, lamp in hand, carrying a bundle of clothes. I couldn't help but notice that she was not wearing a housecoat, only a thin nightgown, which revealed her skin, smooth and golden. "John," she said softly, her eyes bright in the gloom. Her hair hung loose, framing her face with its long, dark waves. "Get ready. Pack everything you own," she said. "Do it quickly. I'll explain later. Gerald will help with the puppet stage. Wash up and put on these clothes. You'll be needing the sweater. Clarissa has a container with sandwiches and thermoses of hot tea and lemonade. You'll be hungry later. It's a long drive to Port Antonio."

"Are we moving house?" I asked, but Mrs. Meitner shook her head mysteriously. "Hurry," she said, "the cars are waiting. Dr. Meitner is already getting water for the journey, as well as for the car's radiators. And, fortunately for us, our driver, Dean, is experienced with the roads and can repair punctured tires, if by chance there's any."

As soon as she left the room, I set about packing. Then I washed quickly with a bar of Pears soap and the water from a blue enamel jug set in a matching basin on my dresser. I dried myself with a towel before changing into the fresh clothes and sweater provided.

I dragged the heavy suitcase to the top of the stairs where, to my surprise, Gerald was waiting.

"Mek me take that," he smiled. "It going go in the first car. My things and Mamma's going in'a the second car 'cause we'a come too."

I was surprised to learn that Gerald and Clarissa would be accompanying us, and wondered how much had been kept from me.

"Gerald, did you know we were travelling today?" I asked suspiciously, knowing now that his possessions were obviously already packed. He was trembling with excitement. "Well, me did know," he said nervously, confirming my suspicions. "But them tell me not to say nothing."

Once downstairs, Gerald and I carefully disassembled the puppet theatre and packed the puppets, while a crew of five black-skinned men moved through the house, carrying and fetching bags and boxes, while taking orders from one or the other of the Meitners. I heard Clarissa's voice in the kitchen giving instructions about her utensils, and I saw Dr. Meitner, dressed in a white blazer, hurry past us carrying a large Spanish jar, usually reserved for storing water during shortages. Then Mrs. Meitner came out on the landing, adjusting her hat, which perfectly matched her pale grey suit.

"Everything alright?" she said, noticing us below.

"Yes, ma'am," Gerald replied.

"We will be leaving soon then," she said, stepping back into her room quickly.

I found the puppet equipment lightweight enough for me to carry on my own. I followed Gerald, arms full, out of the dim drawing-room to the tiled hallway, then through the open front door into the cool dark morning. I never once looked back, for I did not know I was leaving the house for the last time.

Outside the men were loading two cars, which were parked one behind the other, and I saw what I had thought to be a darting light. It was the kerosene lantern the men were using for illumination, being passed from hand to hand.

"Good morning, boss," a balding man in khaki clothes said. "I is Dean, and see that one over there with the picky picky head? Well, that is Cecil, and we is going drive the whole of you to Port Antonio."

The cars looked roomy. I would be travelling with Dr. and Mrs. Meitner in the first car, while Clarissa and Gerald would be in the second with Cecil. I was puzzled about the prospective trip to Port Antonio. Why was so much luggage required, and why was everyone harbouring such an air of secrecy? Having never left Kingston, I was brimming with anticipation, even when I overheard some of the men mention that the rest of the things would soon follow. I sat comfortably in the backseat alongside Mrs. Meitner, feeling as if I had really come up in the world as I leaned against the soft tan upholstery. Dr. Meitner was in the front with Dean, hardly exchanging a word, although every now and again he checked his watch. Then he pulled a pipe out of his breast pocket and stuck it between his teeth.

"Time to go, Sarah," he said. "We've got everything."

By six-thirty, the sun began its journey across the sky, and the cars nosed their way along Duke Street, honking at early morning higglers and market-bound vendors unaccustomed to automobiles. Some higglers stopped to admire the cars, while others waved solemnly as though we were royalty. I tried my best to see Gerald's reaction in the car behind, but he and Clarissa kept themselves well back in its shadows. I leaned forward anxiously when the cars proceeded along Luke Lane. The garment factories were exactly as I had last seen them, dark and ominous, but then there was Madam Hung Chin's shop boarded up and looking dilapidated. I had to swallow hard to keep my emotions in check. South Camp Road was no better for me. I tried to keep my eyes focused on the camp where soldiers were doing early morning exercises, but could not stop myself from straining to see the Chinese school, the walkway, and the large windows of Miss Shaw's house. How wonderful the roses and alamanders looked in the early morning air, heavy with dew and memories.

By the time we finally left the streets of Kingston and the congestion of donkey carts, horse-drawn buggies, bicycles, and push-cart vendors, the roads became narrower and the air sweeter. I became absorbed with watching stray dogs, goats, pigs, and ragged children wander the country road. The vegetation grew dense and tall trees with broad trunks reached toward the sky.

"Is ackee that," Dean said, looking back over his shoulder. "an' those wid the bright flowers is Ponciana." I couldn't help but notice a foul whiff of rum on his breath. "An' that big leaf tree there is breadfruit. The one back so is star apple. It eat nice," he said congenially.

I poked my head out the window to get a better glimpse of green leafy vines that twined around posts and makeshift fences in the bush.

"That is yam," Dean said, "and now we coming up to sugar-cane."

I saw undulating fields and docile Indian cows with enormous sharp horns, chewing their cud and pulling gana ganas as they watched us with large watery eyes, black as ackee seeds. All around us, the air was rife with birdsong.

Coconut palms and sugarcane gave way to banana groves. The skies became grey and the scuttling clouds grew black and heavy with rain. Under Dean's sure hand, the car navigated precarious corners, climbed bravely up small hills, then ascended into foggy mountainous regions, with steep, dangerous precipices. The rain came down in torrents, and what had previously been the road looked like a swiftly moving stream.

"See that down there?" Dean gestured as muddy water splashed up from the grinding wheels. "Is a long drop from here down to Maroon Country."

I was scared on that slippery mountain road. I held my breath and didn't dare breathe until we descended and crossed over rattling wooden bridges at the bottom of the climb. The land fell away again to reveal picturesque rushing streams, waterfalls, hidden coves, and rivers slick with shining silvers and gold borrowed from the returning sunshine.

"What marvellous country, and only three hours from Kingston," said Dr. Meitner, tapping his pipe out the window. "It seems such a shame...."

"This must be the prettiest part of the island," said Mrs. Meitner, her eyes darting to see the landscape on both sides of the road. "And look, Edvard, the view of the sea is breathtaking!"

I, too, sat and marvelled at the splendid Portland landscape, and as I breathed the salt-laden air, it seemed almost as though the solid Blue Mountain ranges leaned down to kiss the sandy shore.

"Let's stop here by the water for our picnic," Dr. Meitner said. "We're almost there."

CHAPTER 8

Gone Abroad

*T*he waves rolled incessantly, then crashed in white-foamed sprays against jutting black rocks where white gulls perched precariously. Hardy palm trees, rooted in sand, leaned their leafy heads toward the distant horizon. Fishing boats bobbed in the hot, dry wind on the aquamarine and indigo sea.

Our cars slowed and stopped at last on the long stretch of a rocky, palm-dotted beach.

"Let's get out and stretch our limbs," Mrs. Meitner said. "Clarissa will set up the picnic. Dr. Meitner and I would like to explore the beach, if we may. And, John, I would like you to come as well since we have not spent a lot of time together."

We walked into the wind, not saying anything. I kicked the sand, examining shells and driftwood, and feeling the sweetness of the warm tide as it washed about our feet. I couldn't help but wonder if they had indeed seen me on the stairs and were now taking the opportunity to discuss it. The knot in my stomach grew tighter, and I was afraid of accusations and innuendoes.

"John," Dr. Meitner began. Then there was a long silence before he continued. "John, it's hard to have to tell you this, with such short notice...." He covered his eyes with his hands in a helpless gesture, as though in pain. "I'm not making a good job of it, am I?" He shook his head despairingly as though it were the most difficult task he had ever faced.

"Edvard, darling," Mrs. Meitner said quickly, "let me tell him."

Her perfume wafted in the air, and the whole world stopped. I waited to hear my condemnation, and my legs trembled in the breeze.

"John," she said in a whisper, "we're going to England, all of us—you, Clarissa, and Gerald, too. We are leaving tonight from Boundbrook Wharf here in Port Antonio and will go over by banana boat."

I reeled in shock from the sudden revelation. It wasn't at all what I had expected, and it felt as though my whole world had crashed.

For the longest time I didn't know what to say. There was only the loud beating of my heart as my eyes burned with tears I dared not shed.

"What about Miss Shaw?" I blurted out, grabbing at straws or anything that would set things right. "What about all the red tape and papers for leaving the country?"

"Everything has been looked after," Dr. Meitner said calmly, staring ahead and hardly daring to look at me. "As for your Miss Shaw," he said with some difficulty, keeping his voice level, "I'm sure Mrs. Arlington will inform her of your whereabouts, won't she, Sarah?"

In spite of his assurance, I felt cheated, betrayed, and angry. How could anyone be so cruel as to take me away from all the things I had ever loved? How could these be the same people I had witnessed caressing each other so lovingly in the dim library? I would have run off then and there had it not been for the thunderous rain, which suddenly came down, sending us running back to the cars.

Because of the downpour, Clarissa was about to repack her picnic baskets when suddenly the sun broke through. Her sad brown eyes met mine knowingly, and I realized we both knew we were leaving Kingston forever. I felt somewhat reassured when her large brown hand secretly squeezed mine.

"Master John," she whispered, "I saved this chicken sandwich specially for you. Food scarce, but my people on Matthew's Lane send a fowl for we goodbye gift. We must honour them and enjoy it, and I want you to have a drink of the Jamaican lemonade I bring in the thermos. We don't know when we going taste it again. May the Lord watch over us all on this journey."

I ate in silence, no longer hearing the roar of the sea, the cry of the birds, or even feeling the sharp lash of the wind.

* * * * *

Port Antonio, the capital of Portland, was a small town with nondescript Georgian wooden houses and one or two Chinese shops, a courthouse, a church, and a market that Dean said was called Musgrove Market. The cars turned off abruptly as we approached the sea.

When they came to a halt, I opened the door and made a run for it before anyone could stop me. I headed toward one of the Chinese grocery shops.

A group of country people were outside on the piazza, idling and passing the time of day gossiping.

"Marning, sar," they murmured as I rushed past. "Beg you a shilling, white boy."

I kept my head down as though deaf to their words and entered the shop. It felt as though I were going home, for I could see the jars of sweets on the counter, the flour bags, the sugar, and the rice, and my heart almost burst out of my chest, for I could almost see Madam Hung Chin behind the counter, smiling.

But it was not Madam, it was a little Chinese girl, who looked about nine years old. She was sitting on a stool, practising counting with some small smooth stones.

"Hello," I said urgently in Hakka. "Hide me, please. Some people are trying to take me away."

She looked at me wide-eyed, and I thanked God that she understood.

"Papa," she called out in English. "A English boy talking in'a Chinese, an' I don't know what him'a say."

"Maureen," the Chinese papa said, laughing, as he came into the room. "English boy dem don't talk Hakka. The boy jus'a play wid you, okay?"

Before I could say another word, Dr. Meitner came into the store behind me, his footsteps light as a feather on the dust-strewn wooden floor. "John," Dr. Meitner said urgently behind me, his voice charged with emotion. I turned around slowly and was inexplicably relieved that I had not spoken Hakka in his presence.

"John," he said coming toward me. He placed his hand on my shoulder before he spoke again.

"I am a very passionate man, John, as you well might know. There is a very good reason why we are going to England. I should have spoken to you about it before, but things were happening too quickly. Please forgive me, John. I sometimes get so caught up in my own concerns and the concerns of Jews like myself that I tend to forget how it affects others. I have only known you a short time, but it is long enough for me to know that you are a good fellow and, John, you are talented, too. I want to give you a chance to make something of yourself. No questions, please. That is just how I am. There are also people in Europe who deserve better from life, and I feel obliged to assist them also, though I am sworn to my promise to look after you. I also know I would be proud if a day comes when you could think of me as your father."

Dr. Meitner was shaking with emotion. I buried my face in his strong shoulder, bit my lip, and held back tears as we walked out of the shop, oblivious to the little girl and her father. We crossed the piazza, neither looking left nor right at the congregated idlers, or noticing the ever-changing turn of the weather. We walked directly to the wharf with the aroma of Dr. Meitner's tobacco wafting in the air.

"You might not have experienced persecution, John," he said, his eyes hardly straying from mine, his every step matching mine. "Persecution is what I'm going to tell you about. It has started to happen in continental Europe. It is no rumour as some others say. It is real. I have seen you reading the newspapers and know that you are well informed about world affairs. My personal mission, John, is to help as many Jews and others as possible before this avalanche of persecution gathers momentum."

"What's happening to Jews?" I asked.

"There are Jews all over Europe, and there are many people everywhere who hate us. It is a unique burden that we carry. Many of us are targeted for crimes of the worst kind you can imagine, and I for one won't be surprised if this prejudice escalates, but before it does, I want to be part of the solution to it, if there is one."

As Dr. Meitner spoke, I couldn't help but recall similar words that Miss Shaw had said about the prejudice against Negroes in America.

I was in a turmoil of thoughts when Mrs. Meitner found us standing down by the wharf in the pouring rain, unmindful of the drenching. She came over with an umbrella, handed it to the doctor, and put her arms around us both, and I felt comforted in her presence.

Two ships in the harbour were being loaded with cargo. I saw their long, steep gangways, and was amazed at how easily labourers came and went along them, though I myself dreaded the inevitable climb.

It wasn't until our luggage was loaded that I saw Clarissa, wearing a Sunday hat, climb the gangway hesitantly with Gerald by her side. They held onto each other for support, and looked back longingly at the land they were leaving behind.

"See?" Mrs. Meitner said pensively. "We will be going on the smaller of the two ships. Clarissa has just boarded with Gerald."

"I'd expected banana boats to be small," I said, sounding foolish as I gazed at the large vessels. "This looks more like a ship."

"Banana boats are actually ships," Dr. Meitner laughed. "They are primarily used by the United Fruit Company to transport bananas and other fruit across the Atlantic, but they do have a few cabins for a small number of passengers. You'll be sharing one with us. It's larger than the one Clarissa and Gerald will occupy."

I couldn't imagine sharing a cabin with them, especially after what I had witnessed, and I wondered how many excuses I could come up with to avoid the proximity.

"I dare say this is the last we will see of Jamaica for some time," Mrs. Meitner said, her eyes welling as she leaned into the wind. I turned away to avoid her eyes, and noticed that the rain had subsided to a drizzle.

A lone dog barked and a donkey brayed, and the air was ripe with buzzing clouds of mosquitoes as the tropical night air embraced us warmly.

Our ship was called the *Victory Morning*. My knees wobbled every step of the way as I climbed aboard, vertigo and nausea not far off. I could see between the slats in the rungs. The seawater swirled far below, causing the ship to heave. It left me dizzy, unbalanced, and petrified. I willed myself to think about all that I was leaving behind, and every glimpse of the dusky Port Antonio landscape, the moored fishing boats, and even the broad curve of the sky above etched themselves into my memory. I wondered if this was what it was like for Madam and Miss Shaw when they first set out on their journeys.

On the wharf far below, strong, black-skinned dockhands, labourers, and crewmen strained under the weight of the precious banana cargo. I heard them singing. At first their voices were equal to the low rumble of the sea, then grew stronger like the mighty waves breaking against the side of the ship, and ultimately the voices revealed a crescendo of rich baritones.

"Come, Mr. Tallyman, tally me banana, day de light an I wanna go home."

And I knew then that I would never forget the splendour of Jamaica.

Part Two

CHAPTER 9

Aboard Ship

A steep flight of steps led down from the deck to a long, well-lit hallway where there were ten passenger cabins. Our cabin was the largest. It had two beds, separated by a privacy screen and a large wardrobe. We had a small private bathroom, as well as a wicker couch, a chair, a low table, and a full-length mirror. Though small, the cabin was cleverly designed to resemble a bedroom with an attached sitting room. There were portholes in each cabin, though it was difficult to see much through them because of the torrential downpours.

I explored the ship from stem to stern in the company of Dr. Meitner, and the crew was more than willing to demonstrate interesting, but complicated-looking machinery in the engine room. More often than not, I spent time alone, holding tightly to the cold iron railings on the sloping deck where I became engrossed with the white-capped waves. Grey clouds changed to white to follow us the rest of the way. And how alone I felt aboard the ship, which seemed little more than a floating cork upon an endless, expansive ocean.

Twilight brought flocks of seabirds, which followed our heaving ship in search of nourishment and roosts.

There were days when I wondered how much longer I could tolerate the journey, for I longed for dry land. My only entertainment was the occasional sighting of sleek dolphins and porpoises in the deep blue water and, once out into the Atlantic, there were sightings of whales. I felt dull, my head ached, and my thoughts were consumed with the plight of Jews in Europe, as well as the discomfort of sharing a cabin with the Meitners. And I clearly recalled Madam Hung Chin's constant fear, which, in my present circumstance, seemed prophetic. Had she not said that I was fair-skinned enough to resemble a Jew, and would be taken away by them? How I longed for a cup of her green tea and her smile to set things right again.

I wondered how Gerald was managing on the journey, but hardly had any opportunity to communicate with him since he and Clarissa remained in their cabin, except during high tea at four in the afternoon when all passengers convened in a room referred to as the "mess."

The meals were bland and soggy, and it was with great effort that I was able to keep anything down.

"Thank the Lord we are provided for," Clarissa said often as she looked hollow-eyed at Gerald, who could barely swallow his portion of runny mashed turnips, green peas, and lukewarm, tasteless cod fillets.

"I hope this is not what we going eat in England," Gerald moaned, sounding ominous, his brown eyes heavy with regret. And all I could do was nod my head in agreement, and took the opportunity to finally speak with him.

"Do you like it aboard ship, Gerald?" I asked. "Have you seen the birds and the dolphins?"

"Yes!" Gerald replied excitedly, then added, "Yes, Master John, me been drawing pictures of everything me see from the porthole, 'cause me don't want forget nothing."

"I don't want to forget either," I replied.

We were two weeks at sea when one afternoon after tea, Mrs. Meitner came to find me on the upper deck where I had isolated myself from the others as I felt I was poor company and also because I wanted to give the Meitners some time to themselves.

The other passengers—four rich Latin American middle-aged men, an aging pantomime actress from Jamaica, and a young Syrian woman from Dominica, who were going to England for one reason or another—had congregated in a circle of deck chairs to discuss their plans, while shading themselves under a large umbrella. I sat alone in the blazing sun on the other side of the ship, away from the comings and goings of crew members, and was startled when Mrs. Meitner joined me on the metal bench where I sat, leaning against an old piece of machinery.

"Are you not feeling well?" she asked, peering at me inquisitively, her eyes as blue as the summer dress she wore under her grey sweater. "You've been keeping to yourself so much lately. Poor thing, you'll feel so much better once we get to England."

I didn't reply and, not wanting to meet her eyes, I focused on the sea and the sky, not always knowing where one ended and the other began, and felt both ill and bored.

"John, darling," she said softly, her pale eyes pleading for attention. "I know how rather awful this upheaval has been for you. However, try to buck up. Time is short, I dare say, and the journey is almost over, so I must at least prepare you for England. Dr. Meitner has told you about the Jewish situation in Europe, but I dare say he hasn't told you everything. I really ought to tell you about myself because it affects us all. Well, John, I used to spend rather a lot of time in my bedroom back in Kingston. Did you ever wonder about that?"

"No."

"Come on, John, weren't you even a bit curious?"

"No."

"I dare say I rather find that hard to believe, for all children are curious. I'll tell you anyway, darling. It is going to come out in the open soon enough. I forge documents, John. I am an artist with a particular talent for forgery and, as you can well imagine, that is precisely how we managed to get you out of Jamaica, through all the required red tape. Look at me. Don't look away, darling. It's nothing I'm ashamed of. I managed in my own small way to help so many people. And remember all those patients who were always coming to see Dr. Meitner? I dare say more than half of them were coming to pick up forged documents, including death and birth certificates. I am paid very highly for my talents. So you see, John, it is not just the doctor who makes us wealthy. We could never have afforded to bring you and Clarissa and Gerald with us on only the doctor's salary. And, darling, the doctor and I plan to put you and Gerald through school in England, if you co-operate. So if I were you, I dare say, I wouldn't want to spoil Gerald's chances for a future."

I was stunned and didn't respond. I sat slack-jawed in the afternoon sun, feeling numb. I wished that there were some way that I could turn the ship around and somehow return everything to the way life had been before the Meitners, but then there was Gerald to consider.

"John," Mrs. Meitner whispered hastily as she got up and dusted off her long skirts, "when we get to England, we will be telling the authorities that your name is George Meitner."

* * * * *

I still wasn't sure what to think of the Meitners, even after their revelations, and I asked myself what Madam would have made of the situation. I could almost hear her reply, for she would have said that the doctor seemed admirable and genuinely passionate about his cause. Mrs. Meitner's attractive appearance and her smooth way of speaking tended to absolve her of her criminal involvement, but there was the good she was doing to consider.

As a result of my personal turmoil, on our last week aboard ship I was even more inclined to spend time alone. My hiding place on the far side of the deck was my refuge. However, one morning, on seeking it out, to my surprise I found the aging Jamaican actress sitting in that very spot. She was going over lines and not paying much attention to my approach. I watched with interest, impressed with how well she used her voice, which was strong and commanding. Her complexion was pale brown, and her wavy black hair was tied back to reveal a pleasant face.

"Pardon me," I said gingerly, coming over to where she sat. "I didn't mean to interrupt."

"That's alright," she smiled, looking me over carefully, then patting the seat beside her. "What's your name?"

"It's John. John Moneague."

"Your name sounds like you must have some French in your background. Are you Jamaican?"

"Yes."

"You don't sound entirely Jamaican, though. Where'd you get the accent?"

"What accent?"

"Well, it's not actually an accent, I guess. It's just that you speak so cultured."

"Do I?"

"Yes, it sounds like you were well brought up."

I smiled, but did not mention my mother's life of poverty, the Chinese school, Madam Hung Chin, or even Miss Shaw and the Meitners.

"Your parents taking you home to England?" she asked, fixing her hazel eyes on me with interest.

"I'm...." I was about to mention that the Meitners were not my parents when something held me back, and I remembered how easy it was to invent circumstances not far from the truth, having practised with Miss Shaw.

"I'm going to go to school in England," I explained.

"What part?"

"London."

"What a coincidence! Well, you must come visit me sometime. My name is Mercedes Williams. You might have heard of me. I perform at the Ward Theatre and spend half the year in Jamaica, but I own a home in London, where I perform in several theatres. Is this your first trip to England then?"

"Yes."

"Poor soul, be prepared to be cold. I'm sure your parents already told you that, although at this time of year, it is somewhat warmer. You'll find that even when it's summer, English people are reluctant to give up their cardigans. I hope you don't mind me saying this, but no offence intended. White people like you will blend right in, in no time."

"I'm not White," I blurted out.

"And the sea is not blue," she replied laughing. "I see you think of yourself as Jamaican first and foremost. I like that."

* * * * *

Mercedes Williams and I found each other's company every afternoon. She told me that the Latin Americans aboard were art patrons on their way to Edinburgh to make a sizable donation to an art museum there. She also mentioned that the woman from Dominica was recently out of divinity school, and was on her way to join her father, a shipbuilder in Southhampton.

Mercedes Williams was enormously entertaining, not unlike Miss Shaw, and it was reassuring to find that she was already on deck, standing in the strong breeze, when we first caught sight of England. "Here," she said, coming to stand beside me at the rail, "this is my address. Don't forget what I said before. Come visit me, alright? I don't want us to lose touch. And you know what? Just call me Auntie."

"Thanks," I replied, not really realizing how large London was, or how difficult it might be to get around.

"Good luck at school," she whispered. I crumpled the piece of paper and quickly slid it into my trouser pocket, for I heard voices and knew that the Meitners, with Clarissa and Gerald in their company, were coming to join us.

"It feel cold out here," Clarissa said, hugging herself in a huge green sweater.

"You'll soon be used to it," said Mrs. Meitner in a voice that seemed to say that was the end of that, but when I looked over at Gerald, expecting to find him shivering, I saw that in spite of the cold, his eyes were shining with anticipation and excitement.

"England at last." Dr. Meitner smiled, coming to stand directly behind me. "I can almost taste it in the air. Our garden will be in bloom, Sarah, but there will be lots to do indoors, with getting the house back in order, not to mention that my practice has to be revived. And, Sarah, your studio awaits you. We will be busy, won't we? And we mustn't forget that these boys will have to be enrolled in school for the next term."

Chapter 10

A New Life

I knew very little about London before my arrival. All I can remember learning at the Chinese school is that it was the capital of England, and that the King lived there in Buckingham Palace. I did not know its geography, or that London, the largest city in the world, was not far from where the English Channel flows into the North Sea. I was ignorant of the fact that the river Thames runs through London and is deep and wide enough in places to support the passage of ships, such as our *Victory Morning*.

From the ship's deck, I excitedly observed several large, busy shipyards along the Thames, where ships, boats, launches, and tugs were docked, and I was particularly excited when the pilot of a small tugboat came to meet us and guided us for the remainder of the journey. Huge factories alongside wharves belched smoke from their chimneys, causing the sky to assume a slate-grey hue. It was indeed strange to see White dockside labourers engrossed with the hauling, pulling, and loading of cargo.

London stretched over a great distance and seemed even larger than my island, though it was hidden in a shimmering mist. Below us dark waves rolled and broke against the sides of the ship. Grey clouds hung low, forecasting impending foul weather. There was the harsh cry of hungry gulls, and the air, heavy with the odours of industry, attested to London's important role in international trade.

As we drew closer to docking, I finally heard British voices, which sounded strange to my ears, for even though I was accustomed to the Meitners, these voices were almost indecipherable, and Mercedes Williams, who had been standing beside me, smiled knowingly, as though reading my thoughts.

"People come here from all over Britain to find work as carpenters, shop merchants, dockhands, and rope makers, just name it, and though they are all British, they all have different accents. Your ear will get used to it after a while. England is where we got our class system, John, so the way a person speaks is a good indication of social class."

"So are these people lower class then?"

"Some are, but not all. You will be surprised how easily you will be able to tell who is a lower-class person and who is not after a while."

"But London also has its opulence, John," Dr. Meitner said, coming to stand beside me, one arm around his wife's slim waist, the other gripping the rail tightly. It was only then that I noticed him, for I had been too absorbed in the new surroundings. I didn't even notice when Clarissa fell prostrate on her knees to thank the Lord for our safe arrival. Only the look of embarrassment on Gerald's face as he tried to hide his eyes behind his hands drew my attention to her.

"Look, Dr. Meitner!" I exclaimed, pretending not to notice the spectacle and at the same time hoping to alleviate Gerald's discomfort. "I've never seen anything so spectacular. Can you believe there are so many ships, and cars, and crowds, and even a train too!" My words sounded stilted and unreal, but it didn't matter. All eyes were on the city, and Gerald was spared.

Dr. Meitner drew closer and he waved his hand expansively. "Take note of the elaborate architecture, John. There are churches, museums, galleries, monuments, theatres, palaces, and so forth. London is the centre of our culture. But don't ever forget that London also has its slums, and that is where many of our fellow Jews are."

"Yes, John," Mrs. Meitner added, "I dare say there are more Jews there than Englishmen. Wouldn't you agree, darling?"

* * * * *

I was surprised that our papers were not questioned by the British authorities and met with their regulations. As far as they were concerned, it would seem, I was indeed the Meitners' son George, who had been residing in the Caribbean with an uncle. I showed no reaction when I was called by my new name, and I noticed that not even a muscle twitched in Mrs. Meitner's serene face. No doubt she was confident in her extraordinary talents, for the travel documents I glimpsed looked professional. Clarissa and Gerald were categorized as our servants, and were granted entry into the country as such.

It was hard to believe that my feet were finally on solid ground after so many weeks aboard ship, and that I was thousands of miles from home. I wondered if it could possibly be the same sun, moon, and stars above us, for I missed home with every breath.

We settled in a section of the city called Chelsea, where the houses were as large as mansions. Our home, Lindonwood House, was a four-storey imposing brick building with broad, worn stone steps at the entrance and a curved drive. The house was situated on a well-to-do street called Cheyne Walk, which looked out on a street lined with tall trees and had spectacular views of the well-trafficked Thames.

Clarissa was installed as housekeeper and cook, and there were four other servants in the household. A plain-faced Irish girl of seventeen, Mary Ambrose, who looked as pale as a sheet of paper with two blue dots for eyes, was to be her assistant. Tom Roy, an elderly, ruddy Englishman with a neatly cut grey beard who always wore a dark suit and cap, was the chauffeur. Raven-haired

Angela Fagan, another Irish national who looked about forty and had the fiercest eyes I had ever seen, was the laundress. Finally, there was Ben Simmington, a Scot recently hired as household handyman and gardener, who was in his late thirties and had a handsome, sunburnt appearance and shaggy brown hair.

My room was on the third floor overlooking the river, while Clarissa and Gerald resided with the other servants "below stairs," as their living quarters were called. The house was spacious, with ornate furnishings, rugs, and paintings on the walls that reflected the Meitners' wealth. Although Clarissa, Gerald, and I were unaware of it, the warm clothes they gave us were second-hand ones that had been donated to a charity.

The three of us were impossibly cold in spite of our newly acquired clothing and were often chided by those in the household who insisted that we should be enjoying the weather. Even the coal fires in the rooms proved deceptive. Once we moved a few feet away from them, we would feel the cold once again. At night we slipped hard clay hot water bottles between our sheets for warmth, but the bottles cooled quickly. I was even reluctant to undress for bathing because I soon learned that baths took a great deal of will power to endure while shivering in damp, cold bathrooms.

* * * * *

I found it unsettling to be in a country where I knew nothing. I did not know the names of the trees outside the windows, or many of the flowers in the garden. I did not even know the birds that swooped down to eat breadcrumbs in the back garden. There were unidentified vines on trellises, and a profusion of scented flowers that I had never seen. I did not know the names of the wildlife or even the insects that shared the grounds.

* * * * *

One cool morning a week after our arrival, I awoke early and crept outside to explore the grounds behind the house. I followed a wide, well-kept grassy path through the expansive garden and through an arbour of tall trees. I heard gurgling sounds. Birds chirped in the branches above and I came upon a small fountain blackened with age, in the centre of which was a figure of a stooping nude female holding a jug, which spilled the gurgling water. Nearby was a stone bird bath.

I felt suddenly sad, being so far from my former life. I longed for even just a glimpse of Madam's shabby backyard of herbs and tangled weeds. I wearily sat down on the edge of the moss-encrusted fountain. I did not notice a potting shed, hidden among the dense foliage of the sheltering trees. Only a familiar voice calling my name made me look up.

"Master John," Gerald said. He hugged himself in a thick navy blue blazer that looked even bluer against his sallow cheeks. "Come inside here. You mustn't mek them see you sad. Them will think you is a gal."

I looked at him shamefaced yet somewhat grateful, for his eyes were sympathetic. "You miss home?" he asked, coming to sit beside me at the fountain. He threw two grey pebbles into its depths.

"Each of these ya stone is a wish, Master John. My first wish is to go back home again. You want to come too?"

"Yes."

"But me want Mamma to be happy, so me g'wane do the best me can to try like it here, even though me don't have no friend. And, Master John, me is 'fraid of causing trouble in'a de people bakra house, so me come out here, but it cold can't done."

"Can't we be friends?" I said boldly, not half realizing that the enormous gulf between us was like trying to cross a canyon with a single step.

"I don't know, Master John, but me feel the Meitner, dem not going like that."

"I don't care," I said, feeling cavalier, "and another thing—you don't have to call me Master John when we are alone."

Gerald shivered and braced himself against the cold. "What was your second wish, Gerald?"

"It already get answer," he said shyly.

* * * * *

One Friday afternoon, when the streets were slick with rain and a heavy mist hung in the air, Mary Ambrose agreed to accompany Clarissa to the market near the High Street on Fulham Road. Clarissa, who was still not accustomed to going out in damp weather, wore a heavy oversized black raincoat that was far too large for her, and tied a bright scarf around her head. She put on a pair of thick-soled, laced-up black shoes that made her look like she was in the army. I looked at her and smiled because I couldn't helping thinking that she would have found it impossible to wear an outfit like that back in Jamaica without a troop of children running behind her laughing.

There was a great deal of excitement in the household among the servants, not only because the Meitners' car was being made available for the trip, but mostly because it would be Clarissa's first trip to an English market. I watched the three of them—Tom Roy, Clarissa, and Mary Ambrose, with large black umbrellas— as they left the house. There was a sudden downpour, and it reminded me that rain in Jamaica was always a good reason for staying indoors, unlike England, where life continued as usual.

* * * * *

On her return from shopping, a wide-eyed Clarissa told us that the marketplace was crowded with vendors and merchants, and that she was forced to breathe musty air from the mingling of wet bodies and drenched clothing. She said there were stalls bulging with used clothes, old furniture, books, and antiques, although there were very few dairy products, vegetables, sugar, and rice, and she couldn't find even one hot scotch bonnet pepper.

She said that without Mary Ambrose's assistance, she would not have known which of the merchants had better value. Merchants solicited aggressively, which frightened her.

"Now, what can I sell the darkie?" A woman, who resembled a gypsy, called out loudly as she fiercely stared at Clarissa. It seemed that everyone turned to see who the darkie was. Clarissa was humiliated. She had never been called a "darkie," and there was no hiding her embarrassment and shame. She lost all excitement and slunk in and out of the crowds, hiding her face beneath her large headscarf.

"Look, luv, you can't be buying everything they's ram down your throat," Mary Ambrose said, steering Clarissa over to where there were a few fresh vegetables. "There'd been a general strike earlier this year, but not to worry. We can still get a couple'a bunches of carrots and turnips, and the potatoes and cabbages look good. We'll be needing a chicken, perhaps some pickled fish, and a dozen eggs. The Missus says we's not to be getting pork or shellfish. Do you think them's afraid of growing claws or a curly tail?"

Try as Mary Ambrose might, she could not get Clarissa to smile, for her heart was clearly no longer in the shopping, and it looked as though she had begun to have regrets about coming to England.

"Don't you be thinking 'bout what that damn fool of a woman said," Mary said soothingly, "'cause I swear on the names of Jesus, Mary, and Joseph that they have worse names to call us Irish."

"But you is White, too," a puzzled Clarissa replied.

"When did that ever matter? Being Irish is a curse in England, if you's to ask me."

* * * * *

By the end of August, Gerald, too, experienced being centred out as a minority. He was labelled a "Gollywog" by passing English children, who chanted "Gollywog" whenever they encountered him, and he told me that on one occasion when he was sent on an errand to the High Street, a little red-haired girl out walking with her mother approached and pointed at him. "Does the black come off him when he washes?" she asked innocently. But her mother was so embarrassed that she apologized profusely.

The children living closest to where we lived were considered "children of Bohemians." Their liberal-minded parents were artists, writers, actors, and poets, who often left them to their own devices, which was precisely how I managed to meet two boys who boldly climbed through the hedge at the back of the property. Curiosity brought them, for the first thing they wanted to know was if Gerald was a cannibal. I was of two minds about telling the truth, but in the end, for Gerald's sake, came clean. Every chance we had, even on the wettest days when tree branches drooped with moisture and the air was a thick, foggy soup, we would meet in the potting shed. My muddy tracks could be found meandering from the terrace through the lush garden, through the trees, past the fountain, and into the shed. Poor Gerald was confined to the house to assist with one task or another, and it was a rare occasion if we ever managed to meet in the garden, for he had become an unofficial houseboy.

As a result of my informal contact with the English boys, I was to learn a great deal about Englishness, and even the names of the flowers and the garden trees, which were rowan and oak. Aside from the roses, which I already knew, I discovered hollyhocks, delphiniums, dahlias, lupines, poppies, and bellflowers.

The English boys—Clive Bates, who was thirteen, and Edwin Charles, a fourteen-year-old—were more than eager to pass on to me what I considered their extensive knowledge. As a result, I became very absorbed with the names of British wildlife, such as stoats, badgers, and moles. However, it didn't take long before it dawned on me that the boys were more than unusually interested in my "parents" and, though naïve, I began to wonder if it had anything to do with the fact that the Meitners were Jews.

"So, John, your father's a doctor, eh?" Clive asked one afternoon, a supercilious expression on his pale face. "What does your mother do besides sleep with the gardener?"

"She doesn't sleep with the gardener!" I exploded. "She sleeps with the doctor!"

There was such a fit of laughter that I began to find them tiresome. Though I kept my thoughts to myself, I couldn't help but wonder if there was any truth in what they had said, and whether it was at all possible that they knew other secrets about Mrs. Meitner.

"She's a flaming artist!" I retorted, but the boys again collapsed into a fit of giggles, and it was then and there that I knew I no longer wanted anything more to do with them.

"Get off of this property!" I shouted, and my voice had such a timbre of authority that it startled even me. "I've had enough of the both of you!"

"She's an artist all right!" Edwin hollered before they both went crashing through the hedge.

CHAPTER 11

New Identities

The first week of September was unseasonably warm. One evening, while we were having supper outside on the terrace, the skies were pink and orange. It reminded me of Jamaica and, inevitably, Miss Shaw.

"Has there been any word from Miss Shaw?" I asked, startled at myself for not having thought to ask before.

Dr. Meitner leaned over his plate, chewed slowly, and between bites of devilled eggs, kippers, and tomatoes, slowly wiped his fingers on a napkin.

"We're lucky not to be in Jamaica just now," he said thoughtfully. "There has been several uprisings on sugar estates, and as a result, all British nationals could be in danger there."

From the corner of my eye, I glimpsed a faint look of surprise on Mrs. Meitner's face as she passed me a plate of rolls, still warm from Clarissa's oven.

"That is rather unsettling," she said. "To think that so recently we moved freely among the natives. I dare say one never knows what to expect in the colonies."

"Well, it's to be expected, darling," Doctor Meitner said. "Jamaica has no trade unions, the sugar cane industry is suffering badly from competition with our European beet sugar, and even their bananas are competing with suppliers elsewhere. Dock workers are demanding better salaries, much as the ones here are, and, to make matters worse, there is not enough money to go around for the few jobs that Jamaicans still have."

"Edvard, that's a thought. I dare say I haven't been following the situation. Sometimes when I'm here in England, with the birds singing and the weather the way it is today, it is almost as though the rest of the world doesn't even exist."

"Come, come, darling, what about our Jews? Are you forgetting? Your heart might be in England, Sarah, but how about your family and mine in Budapest and Vienna? I'm sure John here feels a great deal of attachment to Jamaica, although with the way he has been speaking lately, I could almost swear he was English."

I turned away shyly, focusing on a clump of pale pink roses. Hadn't Miss Shaw said that I had a remarkable flair for accents? Roses always reminded me of her, and like a dog with a bone, I wouldn't let go.

"But have you heard from Miss Shaw?" I asked again.

"Not a word, darling," Mrs. Meitner said, absently playing with the food on her plate with her fork.

"Not to worry, John," the doctor said comfortingly. "I'll get in touch with Mrs. Arlington." With elbows on the table, he clasped his fingers together in front of his lips thoughtfully.

"I have been thinking, John, that it's about time we get a start on the work we spoke about in Jamaica."

"What will I have to do?"

"The first thing you'll have to do is always to address me as 'Sir.' That's the way it is here in England and besides, the young man I'm going to have you impersonate was probably well mannered."

"What do you mean 'was well mannered,' sir?"

"He's dead, John. He tried crossing from Romania into Czechoslovakia by way of the Carpathian Mountains, but he either had a nasty accident or was murdered. I'm supposed to be a relative of his father, who is anxious to get out of Europe. The British are particularly sympathetic to children's causes, so we could use the services of a refugee child to help sway them. That's where you come in, John. His name was Pavel Lawrenski, so that will be your new name for the next twenty-four hours or so. Come, let's go inside. I'll need to show you all the documentation we have on him, which, by the way, you will need to have memorized by this time tomorrow."

We went through an archway into the house, and I caught a glimpse of Gerald, standing at the kitchen door. He was trying to get my attention and hissed. Dr. Meitner was so intent on taking me to his study that he was not aware of Gerald, and there was no opportunity for me to stop to speak with him.

In the study, his large oak desk was immaculate, except for three or four large books left open under the dim light of the sturdy brass lamp. The bookshelves were full of reference books, and two sets of encyclopedias were shelved floor to ceiling along three of the walls. An imposing picture window, adorned in dark purple drapes, looked out over the darkening grounds and afforded a glimpse of the terrace where we had so recently dined.

Dr. Meitner's excitement was evident as he eased himself into the swivel chair behind his desk. Beads of sweat stood out in the creases of his forehead.

"Good, I've got the key," he said, fumbling in his trouser pockets. "I keep everything locked up. It's in the best interest of both of us."

From the desk's middle drawer he removed several sheets of paper before getting up quickly to pull the heavy drapes across the window.

"Just a precaution, if you don't mind," he said, leaning across the desk, his hand shaking visibly. "Even in England, one has to be careful. Now, John, these ten pages are all the personal information I've been given about Pavel, his date of birth, his mother's maiden name, the names of his closest friends, his father's occupation, and some details about the town he came from in

Romania, things like that. Do you think you can manage it? I have every faith in you. And I have also added information about where and with whom you've been staying in England, and how you supposedly arrived here by a small boat after crossing the Channel. Take the papers to your room and memorize them. Our biggest fear, though, is that they might require you to speak a few words in Romanian, but it hardly seems likely, so let's just trust Mrs. Meitner's well drawn-up documents, shall we?"

"Sir," I said hesitantly, "I'm sure I can give it a try, but...."

"But what, John?"

"Well, sir, you did say you were going to put Gerald and me through school, and now here it is September already."

"I'll sort that out, John," he said with a rush as he put away the rest of the papers and closed the large volumes on his desk before returning them to the bookshelves. The only title I glimpsed was *A History of the Jews in Europe* by Harry Goldman. Dr. Meitner returned to the subject at hand.

"John, I have been giving it a great deal of serious thought for some time now," he said, running his hand through his thick hair nervously. "I have decided that it would be best to hire a tutor to come to the house on a regular basis, at our convenience. Because of the work you'll be doing, your frequent absences from a regular school would surely arouse suspicion."

* * * * *

The carpeted stairs at Lindonwood House were quite unlike the ones at the house on Duke Street. They did not squeak, were broad enough to allow two people to walk abreast, and were well illuminated by lamps placed at the foot as well as on the landings. I went upstairs with alacrity, eager to study the document. However, when I reached the landing where the stairs angled and veered off in two directions, I found Gerald silently standing there, pressed up against the wall, as though he were part of the wallpaper.

"Master John," he hissed, a finger firmly planted on his lips. "Me have to tell you something."

The light fell on his face, and his dark eyes appeared sincere and frightened.

"What's wrong, Gerald?" I whispered as he stepped back quickly into the shadow.

"Come with me," he said, practically dragging me toward a small upstairs sitting room. He pushed his weight against the heavy oak door, which opened easily.

"Let we go in," he said. "No one will hear us."

In the rarely used room everything was in place, exactly as it had always been. There were Victorian furnishings, cushions, Oriental rugs, and framed photographs. Only the scented vases of freshly cut delphiniums and dahlias were evidence of recent occupancy.

"Master John," Gerald whispered, "something g'wane on in this house. Them have a printing press downstairs in a room near me and Mamma's room. And is a few night now me see the missus and Ben Simmington go in there. And them take long to come out. Did you know 'bout it?"

I was too stunned to reply and remembered what the boys next door had said: "What does your mother do besides sleep with the gardener?"

"Gerald," I said in a hush, "I can't talk now." I would have liked to talk, but I was pressed for time and weighted down with the tremendous task to be undertaken. I shivered and turned my head aside, worried sick and wanting desperately to set things right.

"I have to do something important that will benefit both of us," I said. "I'm really sorry, Gerald, but I don't have time to explain right now. I'll meet you at the shed in a day or so, okay?"

Gerald turned on his heels, clearly disappointed.

"Don't tell nobody what I tell you, okay Master John?" he said, stopping momentarily.

"I won't tell," I said. "You are my friend, aren't you? And there is no need to call me Master John. We are alone."

* * * * *

The following afternoon, Dr. Meitner and I were driven to an Oxford Street address to testify before a team of immigration officers known as the British Immigration Board, or BIB. It was a particularly cold day. I was wearing a scarf, a cap, thick socks, and a flannel suit. The layers of clothing were not nearly enough to absorb the loud beating of my heart. The scarf at my throat felt warm and comforting and I was grateful for it.

"This is it," said Dr. Meitner as we pulled up to the building. "You are on your own, for once you go before the board, the lives of many others will be in your hands. I trust you have done your homework, and all will go well. And another thing, John, your tutor starts on Monday. Go do us proud."

On entering the building, a uniformed official asked my name and I was given a card with code numbers before being directed up a flight of steep stairs. Dr. Meitner was instructed to remain downstairs, while I was taken through a gallery to a wide room on the second floor with small windows. There were three desks at the far end where I was to be cross-questioned.

Already seated were two heavy-set, unsmiling blonde women, who looked like army officers, and a slim-faced, sympathetic-looking middle-aged gentleman wearing round glasses. I sat in a large and uncomfortable wooden chair in front of them. The room was airless and seemed full of regrets and broken promises. A strange sadness lingered there, which frightened me, and I began to underestimate my talent, though I kept telling myself that I would do well, and that it would be exactly the same as the play-acting that I did when I was with Miss Shaw. Every shift of my feet attracted attention, every cough, every gesture of my hands was scrutinized.

I was questioned over and over again. I took off my scarf and lay it across my lap. Beads of perspiration rolled down my back. And there was no way of knowing if my answers were satisfactory.

"What was your mother's maiden name, Pavel?"

"Anna Bortniak, sir."

"What kinds of work did your father do?"

"He repaired engines, sir."

"And your friend Valter. Do you remember what his father did?"

"He was a tailor, ma'am."

"And your middle name—what was it?"

"Bogdan, sir."

"Very well, which city in Romania is on the coast of the Black Sea?"

"Constanta, ma'am."

"And the closest river to your town?"

"The Danube, ma'am."

After two hours of gruelling questions it was decided that I, as well as my papers, were legitimate. Fortunately, they did not ask me to speak Romanian, and I felt relieved and excited as they shook my hand and congratulated me, informing me that my father, Derek Voss, would be given a pass to enter Britain. I tried to imagine what it would be like to actually see my own father, and I became so emotional that if they had not believed my story before, they certainly would have then.

That interrogation was the first of many I was to undergo in conjunction with the Meitners' cause, and each new wave of Jewish refugees brought with them bleaker news from Europe of rapes, harassments, and loss of jobs, occupations, and properties.

Life for me became a round of constant studying, donning ingenious disguises, visits to the BIB, and the inevitable interrogations. There were times when the cause took us to BIB offices in other parts of London, and even as far away as Liverpool and Newcastle, in order to avoid the possibility of being recognized.

Besides the assistance of Dr. Meitner in various guises, Mrs. Meitner herself was often called upon to be my sister, my aunt, my mother, and even grandmother. By the end of 1927, I could easily count fifty Jewish persons living and dead whom I had impersonated and was directly instrumental in bringing their families into England.

* * * * *

The evening after my first visit to the BIB, Gerald and I arranged to meet in the house after supper. While I was away during the day, he found to his dismay that the shed, where we had planned to meet, was locked. He slipped me a note at teatime, suggesting that we meet downstairs after seven.

Although I was eager to tell him about what had happened at the BIB, I knew I should hold back for the sake of all those others depending on me. I cautiously went below stairs, expecting to find Gerald. When he wasn't there, I took refuge in the pantry, and after a few moments he came in to find me standing in front of a shelf lined with bottles of marmalades and jams that Clarissa had been stocking for the coming winter.

"John," Gerald whispered, inching over to where I stood. "Mek me show you the room. Come." I followed blindly past the servants' quarters and the room they used for eating and relaxing in. It was darker there, and there wasn't much furniture.

"Here it is," Gerald said, easily unlocking the door. "How did you do that?" I asked incredulously.

Gerald laughed softly. "Just a piece of bent wire."

He was right. There was no mistaking the printing press, the inks, the official-looking seals and stamps, and the sheets of high-quality paper. So this is how she does it, I thought to myself.

"We have to get out of here, Gerald," I said sharply. "I have a bad feeling about being here. Promise you won't come in here again. You hear me? Promise."

CHAPTER 12

An American Story

rue to his word, Dr. Meitner hired a tutor, and the upstairs sitting room, with the addition of three desks and a blackboard, became a classroom. Agustus Uriah Brown, the tutor, was a surprise because not only was he American-born, he was a Negro.

He was smiling broadly the first morning when we met him. His broad smile revealed even white teeth, and his skin was as dark as tamarind seeds. He wore a pale blue suit and an impeccable tie. He was a tall man, with low-cropped kinky hair and well-manicured nails. I knew at once that he was the sort of man who cared about the smallest detail. And in his shirt cuffs were a pair of gold cufflinks.

"Good morning, boys," he said tapping his chalk on the newly mounted blackboard. "My name is Agustus Uriah Brown, and I know that you are John and your friend here is Gerald. I'll write my name down for you. Yes, I know you have many questions to ask about me, such as why am I here in England when I should be kicking my heels up in America with the Harlem renaissance there and all."

Mr. Brown sat down on the sofa and patted the seats beside

him. Gerald and I sat on either side of him and listened spell-bound to his story.

"Well, boys," he said, waving his hand in the air. "As I said before, I am from way over there in the old U.S. of A., and so was my pappy, but his pappy was a slave, brought over from Senegal in Africa in the bad days of slavery. My grandfather's name was Osuji, but was renamed Abraham when he was sold to a White plantation owner, Joshua Brown, a supposedly God-fearing man who surrounded himself with slaves who all had biblical names. Can you imagine it, boys? Moses, Isaac, Miriam, and Lazarus all working in the house and kitchen, while Luke, Shem, Cain, and at least fifty others worked in the fields. It was a fine arrangement, the landowner thought, but not so the slaves because he worked them from dawn to dusk, harvesting, planting and dusting, clean-ing and cooking. And there wasn't one of those slaves without calluses at least three inches thick. There was no end to the work-ing day, and no end of lashings if they couldn't hold up.

"On Sundays, a preacher came to the plantation to preach about the value and rewards of hard work. Every slave had to be in attendance, then was sent off to work afterwards for the good of Our Lord. The preacher's name was Reverend Buck.

"One Sunday Reverend Buck brought two runaway slave girls to the plantation and asked the landowner to have some of his finest-looking slaves ready to breed them, in order to multiply his stock. However, unknown to the preacher, the landowner planned to do the breeding himself because the girls were beautiful.

"But that night, when it was as dark as the back of my hand, the landowner made his way, with his gun on his hip, down to the cabin where the girls were held and let himself in. It wasn't long before bloodcurdling screams were heard as he forced him-self on those innocent girls. Both girls became pregnant. I'm sure you know about such things, boys, and one of them bore a light-skinned daughter not unlike you, John, and the other a black-skinned son. The girl with the light-skinned daughter was taken to live in the big house as the landowner's mistress, and the other girl was abandoned to any man who would still want anything to do with her. My grandfather was a strapping young man at the time, but he took pity on the young girl and her child. The slave girl's name was Emma Marie, and they called the child Noah.

"A year later, they had their own child, Ezekiel, who was to become my father. Years later, when his parents were worked to death, Ezekiel followed the underground railway north, and was never to see his brother Noah again. He settled in Windsor, in Canada, and married a black-skinned woman called Charlotte, who had risked her life to keep him safe. I am their son and, boys, I was given the education my grandparents never had. But when I heard my family history, I wanted no part of living in the United States or even near it, and that is why I decided to immigrate to England. It was hard at first, but you know what, boys? My university education credentials served me well, and I want to do the same for you, so I will fill your minds with education, for that is what you need to reach beyond your grasp."

* * * * *

After our morning lessons, which always began with mathematics and literature, Clarissa came with a large tray holding thick soups and sandwiches, followed by trifle, clotted cream, tea, and lemonade. We were so well fed that it was almost hard to believe that there were others in London struggling as a result of scarcities.

Mr. Brown enjoyed the lunches as much as we did. He took the occasion to informally introduce us to American and British literature. Langston Hughes, Zora Neale Hurston, Jane Austen, and Shakespeare were brought to life and discussed at the lunch table. How proud Clarissa was to see her son, a book in one hand and a sandwich in the other, as he took to reading. For pleasure, he read *The Adventures of Robin Hood*, while I read *Ivanhoe*, and then we would exchange books, which resulted in heated discussions between us. My impersonations at the BIB began to feel like unwanted interruptions to my pleasure. Without our even noticing it, time passed and our knowledge grew, and Gerald slowly began to acquire the accent of a West End Londoner.

*****

One morning, Mr. Brown came unexpectedly early. He walked quickly, and there was something quite celebratory in the manner in which he twirled on his heels and waved the morning newspaper at us. There was a look of sheer satisfaction on his face.

"Make note of this, boys. History is being made as we speak! I just read in the paper that there is now a telephone line connecting London and New York. Can you imagine it, boys? Cables under the ocean? And another thing, an American named Charles Lindberg has flown across the Atlantic. What enormous achievements! It calls for a celebration. I'll take you both out for ices this afternoon. Gerald, go tell your mother not to make lunch. Ask her if it will be possible for her to join us, for Londoners will be in pubs raising a pint to progress, while we eat ice cream in celebration. Who knows, boys? Maybe one day we, too, will fly."

"Sir, do you mean to say that we can actually be here in London and speak on the telephone to Americans?" I was thinking of Miss Shaw and our many months apart, and realizing that after all the time I had been in England, she did not even seem to know where I was.

"Yes, John, you can now actually speak to an American from here, though we would have to take the time differences into consideration. But it's more than amazing, and to top it off, my Americans have done us proud by making a moving picture with sound called *The Jazz Singer*. Sometimes I think there is no stopping us Americans."

"Mr. Brown," Gerald said cautiously. "With all of that happening in America, would you be going back, sir?"

The gaiety suddenly went out from his step, and Mr. Brown

103

went to stand by the window. It was a greyish day outside, although the trees looked bright green against the distant silver of the Thames. Tugboats, barges, and small fishing boats were in view, but it was clear that he wasn't looking at them, for he seemed to be staring beyond the horizon, his eyes watery and suddenly sad as he slowly made a fist and punched the palm of his other hand in frustration.

"Not a chance, Gerald," he said softly. "I'll never go back. I have my eye on a prize, right here in London."

CHAPTER 13

The Collapse

I was fourteen years old in 1929, and had been in England for two years. Clarissa said that I had grown tall for my age. I was taller than Dr. Meitner, and even Mrs. Meitner, who was not a short woman, had to look up to me.

"Master John, you going be one tall powerful man when you full grown. Look how the Lord make you big and strapping, and you only fourteen! Good Lord! Gerald, him big too, but him bones still wingy no matter how much me feed him."

Gerald laughed whenever he heard his mother speak like that, and he flexed his bicep to show her how the muscle could bulge to the size of a small orange.

"Mamma," he laughed, "they don't use words like that over here. Not even Mr. Brown, who is not English, uses such words."

"Gerald, you sound like Englishman, and you think I don't know that you never miss a chance to mention Mr. Brown? Him must be your idol."

"I wish he was yours." Gerald chuckled under his breath before returning to his reading, leaving Clarissa to turn her attention to me.

"Master John, I don't know where you is half the time. Dr. Meitner was looking for you. Him never give you a chance to finish one book before him pile you up with a whole lot'a other paper and send you to you room. Him giving you extra lessons?

Even Mary Ambrose notice, and she says him must be trying to get you a scholarship. But don't you work too hard, Master John, you not going be a boy for long, and the Lord want children to enjoy their youth."

I laughed out loud, although Clarissa was right. I no longer felt like a child, and my long-limbed body was proof of my impending manhood. There were muscles in my arms, abdomen, and legs, and I was starting to feel uncomfortable about the knowing stares I received from women, including Mrs. Meitner.

"Yes, Clarissa," I replied unflinchingly. "The doctor demands that I study, but he only wants what's best for me. I want to become a journalist, and the more things I read, the better it is for me."

*****

The weekend after that conversation was to prove the most frightening of my encounters with the BIB. It was a Saturday morning when Dr. Meitner asked Tom Roy to drive me to an immigration office building in Covent Garden. He felt assured that its location on Bedford Street would be ideal for avoiding officers we had previously encountered in other parts of the city. However, I was ill prepared for the interview, perhaps because I was complacent and had only the few minutes in the car to go over the notes I was given.

I was to impersonate Franz Smoljan, an Austrian Jew, who was helping his grandfather Andre and brother Miros to enter Britain. The real Franz had in fact taken up residence in Germany, and was reported missing after the recent reprisals.

Tom Roy had been reading the newspaper earlier and set it down on the seat beside him. He was concentrating on navigating the crowded streets, and I was reluctant to speak with him and distract him. Then it occurred to me that he might be somewhat shy, which would explain why he often kept to himself, except when his services were required. I leaned over the seat.

"Any news in the paper, Mr. Roy?" I asked, nodding at the paper beside him. Tom Roy kept his hands on the wheel, looking thoughtful as we drove from one street to the next, squinting as though searching for turnoffs and shortcuts.

"Yes, Master John," he finally said, "there's lots in the newspaper to fill us with dread, wouldn't you say? There's even news from Jamaica where you're from."

"Really, Mr. Roy, what's the news from Jamaica? More rioting on sugar estates?"

"No, lad, it was something about a lady who was some sort of assistant to the King's representative."

"Mrs. Arlington?"

"Yes, I suppose that was the name."

"What's happened to her? I knew her, Mr. Roy."

Tom Roy pulled the car over, reached for the paper, and searched out the article. It was quite a small one and I wondered if Mr. Roy would have bothered to read it were it not for the Meitners' Jamaican connection. He handed the paper to me. The article said that ninety-year-old Mrs. Arlington had been confined to a nursing home on the island, and was thought to be suffering from dotage and memory loss. I didn't know how to react. I realized, to my distress, that my last hope for a reunion with Miss Shaw had died. I had no desire to share my despondency with Tom Roy, who seemed remote and perhaps unfeeling. I kept a pleasant enough expression on my face, and he was unaware of my true feelings when I thanked him for the information. After all, Mr. Roy knew nothing about my life in Jamaica, or even about the work I was involved in for the Meitners' cause. How then was he to appreciate the enormous responsibility and the courage it demanded, and how was he to understand about Miss Shaw?

"The poor woman is in the best place, I suppose," he said sympathetically, and although he said something else, I didn't even hear him.

Devastated, I sat back in the seat with my head bowed,

avoided his eye, and tried to keep my emotions in check. I tried to divert my thoughts to the school examination I had recently qualified for that would allow me entrance into a London school, reputed for high standards. But I could not feel any joy in the prospect, for as we drove the rest of the way through London's slick early morning streets, my thoughts once again turned to Miss Shaw and Chicago, where Al Capone had masterminded a gangland-style massacre earlier in the year, which the newspapers had referred to as "the Valentine's Day Massacre." I was horrified at the idea that she herself might have been killed. "Keep her safe, Lord," I said to myself, sounding much like Clarissa, and before I knew it, there was no time left for me to prepare for the matter at hand.

* * * * *

To my consternation, when I entered the room where I was to be questioned, I immediately recognized one of the officers. He was the same gentleman in round glasses who had been at my first cross-examination. His ginger hair was greying slightly, but there was no mistaking him. Even the way he sat hunched over his stack of notes was familiar. I was beside myself, thinking that he might recognize me, and for a few heart-stopping moments I was under his close scrutiny until his eyes darted off and, to my great relief, he showed no signs of recognition. He must see a dozen others like myself weekly, I thought. How could he remember us all?

A stern-jawed elderly gentleman in a pinstriped suit also sat at the table. He kept rubbing his freckled hands together, and his small, grey-lashed eyes reminded me of that of an anxious horse, eager for the race to start. He stared fixedly ahead, and took no notice of the woman on his other side, who was youngish, perhaps late twenties, and Chinese, with short bobbed hair, painted nails, and a cold stare.

"Good afternoon, Franz," said the elderly gentleman, leaning forward, a whiff of tobacco on his breath. "I'm Mr. Millar, that's Mr. Henderson, and this is Miss Fong. We are going to ask you a few questions, just so that we can become better acquainted, so let's begin, shall we?" The questions were fired one after another.

"What is your mother's maiden name?"

"What is your father's occupation?"

"What is the name of the street in Vienna where you went to school?"

It seemed all too easy until the gentleman in glasses whispered to the others, then turned to me.

"Please show us the scar you got from your appendectomy."

The request took me off guard. I had no scar and wondered what to do, and I hoped that the terror I felt was not evident in the way I held myself, or on my face, or in the nervousness of my speech. In desperation, I turned to Miss Fong and spoke softly in Hakka.

"Please help me. I need to go to the bathroom." I don't know how I managed to get the words out, for my tongue was heavy and my clammy fingers cold and frozen with fright.

The two men looked at me incredulously, obviously not having understood a word I said. It was difficult to tell if Miss Fong had indeed understood because she looked as serene as before and was unaffected by what I had said. My mouth went dry with fear, and I could barely speak or breathe. Surely I would be exposed as a fraud. Beads of cold sweat dotted my forehead, and I resigned myself to fate.

"Can't you see the boy needs to use the bathroom?" Miss Fong said sympathetically, and judging from the way she spoke, I presumed that she was English-born. "Quite likely, he's embarrassed about his scar, for we all already know that Franz has no appendectomy scar, but if there is indeed a scar, it might be genital, and he might be self-conscious about showing it to us. Let me take him down the hall and show him the bathroom, if I may. I know that if I had a pelvic scar, as he probably does from circumcision, I wouldn't want to show it either. Come with me, Franz. The bathroom is this way."

*****

We walked quickly down a long, dimly lit hall with high ceilings and wooden flooring, our footsteps echoing. I, in my tweed suit, towered over Miss Fong. I couldn't think of what to say. It was as though I was walking toward my own execution. I ran a sweaty palm through my thick, fair hair, feeling as awkward as a child sent to the headmaster's office.

"So, who taught you to speak Hakka?" Miss Fong hissed as she suddenly pulled me across the threshold of an open doorway.

"This, as you can see, is not the men's bathroom. It is my office. Before we return to my colleagues, I would like to know how it is that you know Hakka when you are supposed to be an Austrian? Tell me, are you really Franz Smoljan?"

Miss Fong silently closed the door behind us, and with her back to me, I imagined her eyes to be cold and unfeeling. However, when she turned around, her expression was one of curiosity, so much so that although I felt defeated and beaten, I decided then and there to tell her the truth, even if it meant I would surely have to face the consequences.

"I speak Hakka, because my guardian, Madam Hung Chin, taught me, ma'am."

"Why is there no mention of this guardian in the records we have? Everything that concerns you and your life has been forwarded to us. Your story does not match the information we have. Why?"

"I don't know, ma'am."

"Could it be because you are not who you say you are? Do you realize that you could be involved in a serious crime, Franz? However, I don't know why I'm going to do this, but I'm going

110

to take a rather big risk and go out on a limb. Correct me if I am wrong, but I think you are not Franz Smoljan. There is confidence in your answers, yet there is something about you that doesn't quite fit. It might be that you are involved in some sort of misdemeanour, but in spite of it your Chinese connection intrigues me. I would like nothing more than to get to the bottom of things."

I turned away, wondering how long she would continue to reprimand me before she sent for the police. Outside the sky was heavy with dark clouds. "I respect your brevity," she continued. "Believe me, I know the risks. And you don't have to look so frightened. My parents were refugees. There were riots here in London in the early part of the century against the Chinese when they first came. We were not welcomed, though we worked hard. The British stereotyped us, calling us opium smokers, and even said we were unscrupulous and inscrutable. I am British-born, though my parents brought me up as a Hakka, so I suppose that is why I have always been interested in championing the cause of the persecuted. This BIB position as a government officer has been most opportune. You would be surprised at the difficulties I faced to qualify. Everything seemed to be against me. But as you can see, I managed to do it, didn't I. So you see, Franz, or whosoever you are, you have nothing to fear from me."

* * * * *

Perspiration trickled down my back. I couldn't think of what to say, and like the child I still was, I leaned over and kissed her lightly on the cheek.

"Thanks, ma'am," I said, noticing her eyes soften and a brief smile play at the corners of her lips.

"So what's your real name, Franz?"

"John Moneague, ma'am."

"Co-operate with me, John. I'll have you out of here in no time."

111

Miss Fong returned to the examination room before I did and hurried to her desk to put her documents back in order.

"Gentlemen, Franz Smoljan does indeed have the scar we were told he has. While he was in the bathroom, I surprised him by entering unannounced. I found him standing in front of the urinals. But the noise of the door opening alerted him. He turned around and was horrified to see me. He tried to run away, but not before I saw the scar. Gentlemen, if I were an Englishwoman, I would be blushing."

When finally I re-entered the room, looking somewhat shamefaced, I found the two gentlemen staring at me with bemused expressions, and I was surprised when they told me that papers for entry into Britain would be given to my relatives based on the strong evidence I had provided.

*****

That evening when Dr. Meitner summoned me to his study, I presumed he wanted to discuss the day's proceedings. However, when I entered the dimly lit room, I found an ashen-faced Mrs. Meitner sitting in his swivel chair. The lamp's gentle glow was stark on her pale face, and her blue eyes were distressed. She held her chin in both hands as she leaned against her husband's desk for support.

The room was all at once too still. I found myself straining to hear even the slightest sound that would be reassuring, but there was nothing to alleviate the dread, and even the heady scent of roses from the vase on the desk had become insipid. My first thought was that Mrs. Meitner had become seriously ill, or perhaps it might even be the doctor himself.

I had never seen Dr. Meitner look so weary. His face was a mask of defeat, and even the fingers he ran through his hair

looked puffy and useless. When he waved me toward a chair, it was with a limp hand. It was as though life had been sucked out of him.

Sick with worry, I pulled up the chair.

"John," Dr. Meitner said, nervously drumming his fingers on the desk where the brass ashtray, which he usually kept out of sight, was overflowing.

I focused on two books that the doctor had recently read and left on the desk—*Financial Tables*, a thick black volume, lay across Beard's *Investments*. The pages were dog-eared and worn from use.

Dr. Meitner's manner seemed gentle as he cleared his throat and began to speak, but then his voice became husky with resignation.

"John, you have been like a son to us. I rather regret having to tell you this, but I just informed Mrs. Meitner about something quite disturbing. Believe me, I have done everything in my power to prevent it coming to this, but it is useless, John, absolutely useless. The stock market has crashed in America. As you know, Britain is the financial capital of the world, but we have suffered several debts because of the recent war. Our banks are practically dried up of bullion, which means there's not enough gold to back investments, and the repercussions are being felt everywhere. As a result, John, we are going to lose this house. I simply cannot afford to keep things going. The servants will have to be let go, and we will have to find a smaller house in the East End. With luck, I might be able to continue my practice, but at a considerably lower salary working with refugee organizations. We have a month or two of grace, but if the truth were told, my cause has eaten up what little else we had. Our furnishings and fixtures are up for sale, and we will have to get used to living on top of each other in a small three-bedroom house."

I didn't know what to say, and I didn't know how long I hung my head. My neck ached badly, and I wanted to swallow, but my throat was dry. I struggled to breathe, and heard a dreadful pounding in my ears. It was my heart. When I was finally able to speak, the release for air was exhilarating. I felt like a fish breaking through the surface of ice-encrusted water.

"Sir, what's to become of Clarissa and Gerald, and what about Mr. Brown?"

"I'm afraid Clarissa will have to be let go. She will probably have to return to Jamaica if she cannot find work. I have made some inquiries and with luck, you and Gerald will be able to get into the Jews' Free School near Petticoat Lane Market. There are hundreds of students clamouring to get in. With my connections as a reputable doctor, you both stand an excellent chance for acceptance, better than most others. Many of the students are Jews recently arrived from Europe, who barely speak English and are eager to be anglicized. You have the advantage of already speaking English and there are no fees to cause us concern. As for Mr. Brown, he is well educated and qualified, so it shouldn't be difficult for him to find another position."

I could not believe how cavalier he was in deciding Clarissa's fate, even after he had said so many times before that he did not know how they would manage without her. Did he really think that under the new circumstances, Gerald would be content to remain in England, and what about Clarissa's feelings about returning to Jamaica with nothing accomplished abroad? Dr. Meitner was ignorant of the fact that people would talk and label Clarissa a failure, which she would never be able to live down.

"But, sir," I said, "Clarissa would be in disgrace if she returned home. Please, sir, don't let it come to that, and what about the examinations I qualified for?"

"I'm sorry, John, there is nothing I can do. I have exhausted every option, and now I have the difficult task of telling the servants."

"But, sir, I thought Mrs. Meitner was making lots of money."

"Not nearly enough, John. She has a tendency to exaggerate,

114

don't you, Sarah? Refugees rarely have money to pay for services, and we have also been financing several of the families we brought over, which has caused quite a strain on our reserves. Also, we ourselves need financial backing to upgrade Mrs. Meitner's printing equipment. Things are getting far more sophisticated now than they were even a year ago."

CHAPTER 14

Moving On

Mary Ambrose came excitedly into the upstairs sitting room where I was sitting by the window, watching ships and boats. Despite the crisp, wintry weather outside, the fog had not lifted and I could see water traffic slowly make its way up the Thames by lantern light and, in some cases, generated power. The trees along the walk had lost their lush foliage. There were no customary birds at the window and no gulls over the water, which made me wonder if their absence signalled an impending storm. I searched the skies for black rain clouds, but the fog proved too dense, and there was no telling where the sky ended and the fog began.

"God Almighty! Master John, thar's you sitting daydreaming with so much going on in the house," Mary Ambrose said sharply as she came into the room, startling me. "Everything's packed, not to worry. But me brother Brian's come by from Whitechapel, an' he's bin saying he can find me work in a garment factory over there. Holy Mother of God! I bin so lucky, Master John, 'cause I'll be getting good pay too. Fifteen shillings a week for sewing sweaters!"

Mary Ambrose was flushed with exhilaration, and though I felt happy for her sake, I knew I would miss her and all her exuberance. It is funny, I thought, that it was only now—when she was going out of my life—that I noticed how clear complexioned and attractive she was. Her fair hair, a mass of unruly curls, fell across her eyes roguishly and contrasted with the blue of her eyes. Why hadn't I noticed her? When she came to sit beside me on the window seat, there was no mistaking her mischievous intentions. She pressed close against me, so close that I could feel the warmth of her ample curves and almost taste the coolness of her sweet breath. I tried to move away, but she found it particularly amusing to wriggle closer, and every now and again, a giggle escaped her.

"You'se be best giving me a kiss now, Master John," she said, "'cause Brian and me, we's be going off for our tea, an' I don't know if I'll be seeing you alone again."

I couldn't help but smile at her audacity. I leaned over, intending to give her a peck on the cheek, but Mary Ambrose was not having that. She turned her head quickly and grabbed me by the back of my neck, then planted her full lips on mine. It was an unexpected pleasure, as my whole body throbbed with excitement. We stayed together like that for a good five minutes before she broke away giggling. "Bye, Master John. I'se bin wanting to do that for a long time now. So there, it's done."

I was too taken aback to say a word, and even after she hurriedly left the room, I still felt the pressure of her lips on mine as I traced the outline of her kiss with my fingers, marvelling. Is this what it is like for the Meitners, I wondered.

*****

Tom Roy, too, came to say goodbye. He was obviously feeling awkward about leaving the house and family. He assured me that he was content with retirement, but there were tears in his eyes, though he said he was looking forward to sharing a seaside rose cottage in Cornwall with his retired sister, Gertrude. I shook his hand as he tipped his cap to me.

"It was a pleasure, young John," he said, barely hiding the tear on his cheek. "Come see us if you can."

I went out on the terrace to look at the garden, trying to remember how it had looked in the spring and summer, riotous with roses and all the other flowers in full bloom, but the day was wintry and cold, and the garden had gone to sleep. I pulled my muffler tightly around my throat, hardly feeling the damp and the dreariness. A few birds had come to pick at the breadcrumbs we had left for them, and I wondered what would become of them when we were gone. I listened to the silence in the garden and walked its full length, twigs breaking under my feet, and fondly remembered what it was like the first time I had seen it.

My eyes were watery with tears as I buttoned my jacket and approached the copse. The trees seemed almost conspiratorial, standing together in the silence as though watching and wondering. The fountain and the bird bath were long dry, and when I looked expectantly into the bottom of the fountain, I found dried moss, dead leaves, snail shells, and small grey pebbles, and I remembered Gerald's wishes. I covered my mouth with my hand to prevent sobs from escaping and held back tears.

Then I saw the little shed among the trees. It looked somewhat neglected. I went over and leaned against the window. Quite unexpectedly, I heard a voice. I immediately assumed it was Gerald, but something in its timbre prevented me from calling out to him. Then I heard it more clearly.

"What's to become of us now, my darling?" a male voice said, and the sound of it was so charged with passion and longing that I couldn't help but wonder who might be saying such tender words. I instinctively became as silent as possible, and avoided the crackle of leaves, the snap of twigs, and the swatch of dry rustling grass near the shed. Taking a chance, I peered in through the window, heart thumping.

What I saw that day in the shed's dimly lit interior has lived forever in my memory. Somehow, even more so than Mary Ambrose's kiss, it marked the moment when I knew I was no longer a boy.

At first I thought the person inside might be Dr. Meitner

because of his height. On closer scrutiny, as I looked through the dusty windowpane, I realized that unlike Dr. Meitner, these bare limbs were muscular and the skin was smoother. I couldn't see the man's face, though some clothes that lay in a tidy heap nearby appeared to be workmen's clothes. Whoever it was, he was quite unaware of my presence, being occupied with a woman in his arms. I couldn't see the woman's face either, for the two people were much too close together. But then I heard a moan, and the woman arched her body and turned her ecstatic face toward me. I caught my breath sharply, recognizing her, and was terrified of being discovered. There was no mistaking the wavy dark hair and the cornflower blue eyes of Mrs. Meitner.

I cannot remember running through that cold winter garden, trampling the vegetation in my wake. All I remember is my fear and regret and remorse from the trauma of being exposed to such illicit intimacy. As I ran, I prayed that the trees, though naked and bare, would succeed in keeping me well hidden. And what would I say to Mrs. Meitner when next I saw her? And what would she say to me?

I also remember the tremendous bang the french doors made when I let myself into the house, and what a relief it was to catch my breath and lean against a side table near the doorway. I caught a glimpse of my face in the mirror hanging above the table. Two bright red splotches stood out on my cheeks. There was a wild look in my eyes, and my hair and clothes were dishevelled.

*****

Angela Fagan came in from the pantry when she saw me looking in the mirror. She was smiling.

"All the wee girls must be chasing after you, with your good looks and all," she said. "Is a good job you'se a fast runner, 'cause I seen you just now, shooting like a Banshee through the garden. It sure's a grand day for running about, is it not?"

I laughed. I had not had much to do with Angela, and had not realized she had a sense of humour.

"When will you be wanting your tea?" she asked. "I'll be leaving after—going back to Ireland, you see. I'se been offered a post looking after two little ones in Belfast. Had enough of England as it is. Since I have no family here and no friends to speak of, going back will be a treat, don't you think?"

"I won't be needing tea. I'm going down by the river for a while."

What I wanted to do was get out of the house. I wasn't at all ready to face Mrs. Meitner. And though the weather was colder than I would have liked, I wouldn't mind it. Although I was dressed warmly, I took an extra scarf from the scarf rack and pulled on a cap.

"Glad to hear you got a job in Belfast," I said. "I hope it works out. Good luck."

"Thanks, Master John. Seeing as I never did have young ones, this is probably my one chance to be able to look after wee ones."

She fetched a vase of roses from the pantry then, as though from force of habit, began to dust the cedar table by the window. She held her head down, appearing industrious, though her eyes were swollen with tears, and I wondered if this household was the closest she had come to having a family. I couldn't take my eyes off her strong reddish hands as she dusted and did not notice when Mrs. Meitner came in. "Oh there you are, Angela," she said cheerfully. "Do you mind running a hot bath for me before you go? I dare say it's been a long day, and with us closing the house and all, I rather think that it is entirely too much work for a body."

"Yes, ma'am. My bus leaves in an hour, and then there's the ferry to catch."

"I dare say you've got lots of time, Angela, and if you miss the bus, the doctor will drive you to the station. I'll just run upstairs and get my toiletries together."

To my relief, she spoke as though I wasn't even there. It was not until I went toward the pantry, intending to find Gerald, that she let her eyes rest on me.

"Everyone's busy, I dare say. Are you all packed, John? Will you be taking that old puppet stage from Jamaica? You're far too old to be wanting it, but I know how easily one gets attached to things. I'm that way myself. I even get attached to people, whether that's for good or bad."

I couldn't meet her eyes, for though she herself might not have been aware of it, her words were full of double meanings. I gave no indication of my thoughts. I looked away from her, and saw the vase that Angela Fagan had brought into the room earlier. Beautiful pink long-stemmed roses were carefully arranged with dried ferns as an accent. They were a loving gift from Dr. Meitner, who had wanted to appease his wife about the move. Somehow, my usual pleasure in seeing roses was no longer there.

"All my things are packed," I mumbled. "The stage, too. Perhaps I'll find some use for it. If you'll excuse me, I was looking for Gerald."

"Well, off you go then, John. I rather think Gerald will be pleased hearing about going to the Jews' Free School, don't you?"

* * * * *

I went below stairs to find Gerald and Clarissa in prayer. Their room was bare, and even the sheets were removed from the beds. In fact, it was so spotless there was no sign of their recent occupancy. Seeing me in the doorway, Clarissa rose from her knees, looking weary, her eyes sad.

"Master John," she said, "I thought you gone with the others. The house sound so quiet, me did think it empty. Dr. Meitner gone go look at the new house, and him must'a take him wife 'cause I don't see her, an Mary Ambrose gone out for tea. Is only Angela was here, but she leaving soon. You looking for Gerald?"

121

"Yes."

Gerald seemed embarrassed that I found him on his knees, but quickly got up and sat down on the bare mattress, his dark eyes unfocused. I could well understand his despondency about the future, for in many ways, I felt the same way, too.

"Hi, John," he said, sounding exhausted and barely looking up.

"Gerald," I said, hoping to reassure him, "at least you'll be going to school, and I'll be there, too."

"But what about Mamma?" Gerald retorted. "They're bound to send her back home, even after all the hard work she's done for them. That's why I don't trust anyone but family."

"Do you think of me as family, Gerald?"

"I don't know what to think, John. I guess you're different, but you're also White like them, aren't you?"

"Gerald, I am going to tell you something that might surprise you. I am not White! My mother was a mixed-blood, Coloured Jamaican. It was my father who was White."

Clarissa chuckled softly. "You sure look White to me, though. You must be what them call 'Jamaica White.' Anyway, enough of this nonsense 'bout colour. We did just say our prayers, and only a miracle can change things now."

* * * * *

Mary Ambrose came dashing downstairs, bursting with excitement. She barely stopped a moment to hang her coat and hat before coming in search of Clarissa. "Clarissa!" she called out urgently, making a beeline for their room. "Clarissa, I'se back from tea. You won't believe what me brother's bin saying."

Mary Ambrose smiled when she saw me, and immediately plopped herself down on the other side of the bed with Clarissa. She was so excited, she was waving her hands in the air, her thick hair bobbing up and down.

"Jesus mercy! Brian says you'se can get work at the garment

factory, too, Clarissa, sewing sweaters like me 'cause he's gone and spoke with the manager, and the manager says they'll be needing loads of help. Can you'se believe it, Clarissa, I'll be dead happy for us both working side by side again! I hope you don't think I'm a right pain."

Clarissa burst into tears. "Heavens be praised, thank you, Jesus," she kept saying over and over until finally she covered her face with her work-worn hands and wept as Mary Ambrose put an arm around her reassuringly.

"No need to cry, Clarissa," she said soothingly, "God Almighty! We's bin good friends, and all of us going to be staying tonight at a lodging house on Middlesex Street, near Whitechapel Road. Our Brian's arranged it. Want to come, Master John?"

I looked at her luminous face and couldn't help but smile. The memory of our kiss still lingered.

I would have done anything to go with them, but I still wasn't sure what the Meitners might think, and after the incident in the garden, I was still rather shaken.

"I was actually going to go for a walk down by the river," I said reluctantly, "and I was wondering if Gerald would come."

"Why don't we's all come?" Mary Ambrose suggested brashly. "It's our last day here, too. Jesus, Mary, Joseph! I look an awful fright. I'll scare off robbers, won't I? When we's get back, we can get we selves ready to go along to The Mustard Bowl—that's the lodging house—if you don't mind."

* * * * *

We didn't see anything down by the river that we had not seen a hundred times before, but the evening air was crisp and fresh, and the waves were particularly choppy. The wind picked up the farther we walked, and moored boats swayed drunkenly. River men in oilskins carried lanterns, signalling each other from the decks of small craft and barges, and the low sound of the horns made me feel lonely. I was glad of the company, for with

Clarissa's laughter and surefooted Gerald beside her, not to mention Mary Ambrose, who was startled even by the buzzing sounds of insects and the unexpected flapping of seagull wings, I felt less lonely. And when we looked back at the long way we had come, it was somewhat comforting to realize that we had passed through so much together. High above us, the lights of the city winked. Other people were walking along the river that night, but for me it was almost as though they were not there. Mary Ambrose linked hands with Gerald and me, and sang a song about leaving home, and if I didn't know myself better, I would have cried.

It was nine-thirty before we wearily returned to the house. We were just turning into the driveway when Dr. Meitner arrived home in his car. He slowed when he saw us, and when he got out, he stood by the entrance briefly, looking up at the tall narrow windows. The house was unusually dark.

"You've been walking, have you?" Doctor Meitner said cheerily, addressing none of us in particular as we drew abreast of him. "It's a nice evening. I've been at the new house. It's in Stepney, near Regents Canal. It's not a bad place really. It needs some work, though, and it will take some getting used to. I took some things over, just small things. I didn't intend to stay this long, but then I hung some pictures and wallpapered the living room. It looks quite cozy, and before I knew it, time was passing me by."

"Clarissa has found a job," I said excitedly, using that information to explain why I was spending time with the servants.

"Really? Where will you be working, Clarissa?"

"I'll be working with Jews again, sir, in a Whitechapel garment factory on Commercial Road."

"Splendid," Dr. Meitner said as he turned his key in the lock to let us in. "And what about you, Mary, any news?"

"Yes, sir, loads of news. I'se going to be working there, too. Isn't that right grand?"

CHAPTER 15

Changes

The house was unnaturally still—too still, and the rooms were darkened. Clarissa and Mary Ambrose went to fetch candles and lit the lamps on the stairs. Dr. Meitner bid us all goodnight and went upstairs. As I watched his elongated shadow, I was full of memories of Jamaica.

"Will you be coming with us tonight?" Mary Ambrose hissed, brushing against me as she hurried past, taking a lamp for the doctor. There was no time for me to reply. The house suddenly erupted. The doctor was screaming and it sounded as though the Day of Judgment had come.

"Hurry, bring a lamp! The carpet's all wet up here, and the bathroom door's locked from the inside!"

We all charged up the stairs, taking them two at a time, and when Mary Ambrose held her lamp high, the shadows receded to reveal a pool of blood seeping from beneath the bathroom door.

Mary Ambrose covered her mouth and held back a scream. Clarissa steadied the doctor, while Gerald and I broke down the bathroom door.

* * * * *

There was blood splattered in the washbasin, on the floor, and in the tub. The window was ajar, cold air blew in, and bloody

125

hand marks, like snail trails, were all over the wall, and when we stepped behind the partition where the toilets were, we found them.

A nude Mrs. Meitner was lying on the cold floor, her knees drawn up to her chest, her splayed arms covered in deep, bloody slashes, and blood oozed from a large, grotesque wound in her abdomen. Her hair was dishevelled around her pallid face, which was turned toward us, a mask of horror. Her eyes were wide with fright, and her mouth was opened from screaming. Ben Simmington was lying across her, fully clothed, in a blood-soaked jacket. In his lifeless hand he clutched a revolver, and on the floor beside them was a sharp blade the doctor often used for shaving.

"God Almighty! I'll call the police!" Mary Ambrose shouted, dashing down the stairs, leaving the rest of us to console the doctor.

"Sarah, Sarah, my darling Sarah! What has happened here, Sarah? I love you, my dear angel, I love you."

For the longest time it felt as though everything around us was unreal. Clarissa removed her apron and respectfully covered their faces. Dr. Meitner, on unsteady feet, moved closer to adjust his wife's hair, which spilled out from under the apron.

"Don't touch anything, Dr. Meitner," I said, sounding somewhat too harsh. "The police will want to examine everything."

It wasn't long before we could hear the sounds of sirens, wheels squealing, and a shouting crowd running along the pavement outside. Between us, Gerald and I managed to support the doctor, for he had almost fainted. We made it to the downstairs sitting room as he babbled in delirium, and Clarissa went to the front entrance to let the police in.

"May the Lord have mercy on us all," she sighed.

* * * * *

None of us spent the night at The Bowl of Mustard. We were called into the police station for questioning. It was seventeen hours before it was decided that Dr. Meitner needed hospital bed rest, and the police established a motive and a murderer. Apparently Ben Simmington had carried a note on his person that read:

Dear Ben,
This is the last time I will be able to afford to pay for your services, wonderful though they were. The house is being sold, and we will be moving to a much smaller home. I will no longer have an income of my own, so everything, sadly, must come to an end.
                    With many thanks.
                    Sincerely,
                    Sarah Meitner

The police theorized that Ben Simmington had intended to rob the house on the assumption that it was empty. They said he climbed in through the bathroom window and surprised Mrs. Meitner at her bath, then raped her. From the wounds on the bodies, they surmised that she had put up a valiant fight, slashing him with the shaving blade, but in the end was no match for him. He shot her to silence her, then panicked over what he had done, and shot himself through the heart.

I didn't know what to believe, though I knew their conclusions were not totally accurate, and have often wondered if the lovers had had a bitter quarrel over their impending separation and perhaps even over money that Mrs. Meitner must have been providing. I kept the incident of their tryst in the garden to myself, for I had no desire to bring notoriety to Mrs. Meitner's name.

* * * * *

It was sad, but she was never a mother to me. For all the years I knew her, Mrs. Meitner had been a remote figure on the periphery of my life. She never seemed to have her heart in anything, not even the Jewish cause, and my own conclusion was that she did the work solely as a source of extra income. Her death brought the realization that Dr. Meitner genuinely cared for me—that I was more than just a useful accomplice picked up off the streets of Kingston.

"John," he said from his hospital bed, his lips white, his arms frail and trembling. "If you need anything, anything at all, let my lawyer know. Thank Clarissa, Gerald, and Mary Ambrose, and if they have nowhere to go, feel free to have them remain with you in the new house. They have proved themselves."

He reached out and held me in his arms.

"I trust your judgment, John. You have been everything I thought you would be. Sarah … my beloved Sarah and I were so proud of you."

* * * * *

The newspaper headlines screamed "Murder in Chelsea" or, in some cases, "The Gardener Did It!" and even "Doctor's Hands Bloodied in Vicious Murder." Our every move was scrutinized. There were photographers at the funeral and even at the hospital where Dr. Meitner returned after the service. London couldn't seem to get enough of the story. Photos of the Meitners were in every British newspaper and tabloid, accompanied by an old photograph of Ben Simmington, taken when he was twenty and looking like a country bumpkin.

Everything seemed to fall around us like a house of cards. Whatever was left of the furnishings was hurriedly cleared out of the house, and many fine pieces, which we could not accommodate, were sold in an estate sale. Dr. Meitner's lawyer, Mr. Bernard Hollingshed, a fussy old man with receding hair, sagging jowls, foul-smelling breath, and a reputation for being somewhat unscrupulous, was in charge.

"I've decided," Gerald said, a week after the murder, "that I want to study the principles and practices of accounting and economics, because after seeing what happened to the Meitners, I am convinced they were using money foolishly, and perhaps for something other than what we have been told. Can you imagine it, John, going from being comfortably rich to how it is now? Where on earth did their money go?"

I looked at Gerald, as though for the first time, and saw to my amazement that he had grown tall, handsome, and strong in his limbs. What a long way he had come from the ragged boy whom I had first seen playing with a rusty iron wheel. Seeing him as he was now, looking assured and confident, left no doubt in my mind that he would achieve whatever he set out to do. In spite of his metamorphosis, I had kept information about the Meitners' activities from him not only because of his station, but because I could not betray the Meitners' trust.

The two-storey, three-bedroom house on Mile End Road was larger than many of the other residences in the neighbourhood. Like the others, its latticed windows did not overlook a garden, only a narrow patch of dirt at the back and the dusty pavement in front. There was no driveway or a garage, for the houses were situated too closely together. Dr. Meitner's expensive car would have looked dreadfully out of place. There were no trees or shrubs, only a wasteland of rundown buildings and homes in general need of repair.

One Wednesday morning, a week or so after we moved in and Clarissa and Mary Ambrose had already left for work, Gerald and I were in the kitchen eating pork sausages and fried potatoes. The aroma hung deliciously in the air. Neither of us said anything about food shortages, or even the lack of storage space in the house. Nor did we suggest ways to alleviate the crush of Clarissa's pots and pans temporarily piled one on top of the other on a side table. It was such a pleasure to have free reign in the kitchen. I had not cooked a meal since leaving Jamaica and besides, Dr.

Meitner would be returning home the following day. It felt almost sacrilegious to eat pork, even in his absence.

"What do you think of Mary Ambrose?" Gerald asked out of the blue, waving his fork, then carefully tracing her curves in the air.

"She's alright, I guess," I replied, tactfully not mentioning our kiss.

"John, she can sure make corn beef and cabbage, and though this old cooker is more ancient than any I have ever seen, she can do wonders with it."

"Really? I thought your mother did most of the cooking."

"Yes, you might be right, but John, have you seen her eyes? They're like sapphires."

We sat in silence at the mahogany table with its matching chairs and sideboard from the Chelsea home. The furnishings added an air of elegance to the room, not unlike that of a beggar woman wearing a mink coat.

Gerald leaned over his plate, examined his meal, then set aside his fork. His shoulders slumped and worry lines were visible on his forehead. A deep sigh escaped him. It sounded so hollow and forlorn that it sent an unexpected shiver up my back.

"John," he said huskily, "you know I'm only just talking about Mary Ambrose to get my mind off things. You realize that, don't you? Sometimes when I think about what we saw that night in the Meitners' house, it makes me so sick I don't even want to eat. When I think about what can happen to people—real people that you and I know—it scares me. It really breaks my heart, John. I don't know how I even manage to get through the day, and I don't know what will happen to us when the doctor comes to live here."

I put aside the heavy skillet, wiped my hands on a dishrag, and went over to Gerald. I was as frightened as he was, though I was unable to speak about my fears. I reached out tentatively, rested my hand on his shoulder, and felt him shudder at my touch. He turned his head aside, perhaps so that I would not see his tears. I choked mine back, and Gerald and I hugged each other like brothers, finally surrendering to grief.

We were having a drink of cocoa when the front door rattled. I thought perhaps it might have been Clarissa or Mary Ambrose. I was wearing slippers, a robe, and flannel pajamas when I opened the door. To my surprise, Mr. Brown was standing on the steps, carrying a bunch of yellow roses and a newspaper, his coat buttoned to his throat against the cold.

"Hello, John," he said, his voice low and sympathetic. "May I come in?"

"Why, hello, Mr. Brown. What a surprise. Come in. How did you find us?"

"It wasn't easy, John, but since I have the privilege of being tutor to yourself and Gerald, Mr. Meitner's lawyer felt obliged to inform me of your whereabouts. I mentioned that you were perhaps too preoccupied with other things, and had neglected to pass on information about your new residence."

"Good, sir, and you were right, too. The doctor is in hospital, and we have been trying to cope on our own. Come in, Mr. Brown. The sitting room is this way."

"First, John, let me say how sorry I am to hear about what happened in Chelsea. It was a terrible, terrible thing, and when I think about how much worse it could have been...."

* * * * *

The sitting room with its few furnishings—a small sofa, two chairs, a rug, and a side table—looked spartan compared to the room Mr. Brown had last seen us in. He walked in, as jauntily as always, before stopping to examine each of the four paintings on the walls. All were English landscapes, except for one of a nude. Her back was turned away modestly as she gazed toward a distant European wood.

"This painting is called 'The Green Nude,'" Mr. Brown said enthusiastically. "It is reputed to be over a hundred years old and was painted in Austria. No doubt it is valuable. I can see why the Meitners were fond of this piece. They were Austrian Jews, you know, and this figure must have somehow represented them. They came here threadbare, with almost nothing, then made something of themselves, acquiring property and possessions, even as they looked back lovingly to the Vienna Woods. I saw this painting before at the other house and admired it. Imagine owning a painting by Ignacio Douglasi and living around here! Anyway, the real reason for my visit is that I have been wondering what has become of Clarissa and Gerald."

"They're here with us, sir," I replied, noticing the look of pleasure in Mr. Brown's eyes. His eyes followed me eagerly, noting my slightest gesture, the curve of my arm, and the way I stood, and even the way my hair fell over my eyes.

"Someone's been cooking sausages," he said, sniffing the air before taking a seat.

I rested my mug of cocoa, which I had been gripping all through our exchange, on top of the fireplace mantle. I was so self-conscious about the house that I saw the fireplace as an ugly blackened creature that devoured coal, and I hoped that Mr. Brown would not notice that the grate needed cleaning, or that the soot-stained walls had been long neglected.

It was some time before he spoke, for his eyes swept the rooms expectantly. He looked toward the dining room, the kitchen, and the stairs, and then back out the window, where weak sunlight shone in.

"So Clarissa and Gerald are here," Mr. Brown said, beaming. I was sure that he did not notice anything, not even the cold air seeping in, or that it ruffled the fringes of his long scarf.

"Gerald's in the kitchen having cocoa," I said hastily. "It's drafty in here. We plan to stuff the cracks in the walls with rags until we can repair them properly and, by the way, Clarissa's found work sewing sweaters at a factory with Mary Ambrose."

Mr. Brown looked somewhat disappointed as he laid the bunch of roses on the side table and allowed me to hang up his thick coat.

"These roses are for the house," he said solemnly. "I remember how much you all enjoyed having flowers. It would be nice to see Gerald. Would you let him know I'm here, John? I hope he has been keeping up with his studies."

CHAPTER 16

Miracle among Monuments

T here was no mistaking the pleasure on Mr. Brown's face when Gerald came into the room. He threw a big arm around him and gave him a hearty hug.

"Good to see you," he said, clapping Gerald on the back before going over to the window to look out through the rain-streaked panes. "When's your mother coming home, Gerald?"

"Around three, sir."

"Splendid! I'll come back then. Now if you'll both excuse me. It was a pleasure, but I must be going."

* * * * *

Gerald and I shared a bedroom with a sad view of our deteriorating London neighbourhood. Several smoke-belching factories were nearby, and the very air was sooty. The walls were thin and it was possible to hear even the slightest toss and turn from Clarissa and Mary Ambrose's room next door. Every now and again the whole house shook from the rumblings of passing trains and automobiles.

Industrious Jews in the area sold food, clothing, and household items from makeshift stalls, pushcarts, and even suitcases. Most of them managed to get by without speaking any English, and it was not uncommon to hear Russian, Ukrainian, and Yiddish, and to smell the pungent odours of cabbage rolls, gefilte fish, potato soup, and borscht in the air.

It was a different world than Chelsea. There were no fine gardens, museums, and upper-class high streets. These narrow streets were crowded with beggars, seamen, pickpockets, prostitutes, the poor, and European refugees who jostled the sidewalks alongside those others lucky enough to have found employment, such as Clarissa and Mary Ambrose. It was from English-speaking Jews that Clarissa and Gerald finally heard word about the plight of the Jews in Europe. Both were left wondering what they could do to help, and both speculated whether the Meitners had done anything to help their people at all.

As a result, Clarissa squirrelled away a few shillings of her earnings to give to the Jewish cause. She wanted to donate it to the synagogue, but feared being talked into conversion, so she went to Saint Dunstan's, a local church, intending to inquire about donating to the cause. The church, with its tower and ancient walls, reminded her of a castle amid its humble Stepney surroundings. The churchyard also included a burial ground with stone monuments and tombstones.

Clarissa stood beside one of the tombstones that bore a simple wooden cross with the inscription "To fall asleep is not to die. To dwell in Christ is better life."

That is where Mr. Brown found her, lost in thought, unmindful of the mud beneath her feet and the soggy pathway her boots had made.

"Clarissa," he called softly, stepping lightly across damp grass. Already he could feel winter's chill in the air as a cool breeze brushed against his cheek.

Clarissa pulled her scarf tightly around her face and looked around. Suddenly she saw Mr. Brown standing among the graves, and her eyes widened with surprise.

"Oh, is you, Mr. Brown. You give me a fright, 'cause for a

moment me did think it was duppy calling me. I only hope you is not a duppy. How you know where to find me?"

"Clarissa, what a pleasure it is to see you again. Please call me Agustus, won't you? And what in heaven's name is a duppy? I went to the house for the second time today, and Gerald informed me that you were on your way here. Do you know how lovely you look on this wet afternoon?"

Clarissa smiled shyly. Her boots were splattered with mud and her coat didn't quite fit. She had started to wear her thick black hair loose rather than pinned up in braids, and it peeped out from under her scarf. She was not at all used to being complimented, but welcomed it.

"Thanks, Agustus. Is nice to see you too, but Gerald have no business telling everybody where me is. But since is you, it okay. But how come you don't know that duppy is ghost? Everybody back home know that."

"There's a lot I don't know about you, Clarissa, and Jamaica, where you're from. But I would really like the chance to know more. Perhaps you can teach me. Clarissa, you look so beautiful, it is hard for me to resist holding you in my arms. Come, come, you don't have to look so frightened. The last thing I want to do is scare you off. Forgive me, but it's not easy getting down on one knee here in the cemetery, but I want to ask you to marry me."

"Mr. Brown, you know I can't go marry you just like that. I have things to consider. There's Gerald for one, and the doctor not too well since the murder, and who going look after Master John?"

Although Clarissa protested, her words were ineffectual. Mr. Brown's proposal was nothing short of a miracle, though she had a great deal of difficulty coming to terms with the reality of it.

"Stop," she said softly. "You're not supposed to want me. I'm only a housemaid, and you is a professor. I have never been anything else until now that I work in the factory."

But Mr. Brown would not be deterred. He drew closer, put his hand on his heart, and spoke softly as though every word were precious and every gesture memorable.

"My dearest Clarissa," he said, "is that how you see yourself? Well I see you as a woman who was brave enough to cross the ocean, to make a better life for herself and her boy. What do you mean, 'only a housemaid'? Yours is a humble but honest profession. And you rose above it, Clarissa. You became a housekeeper in charge of a large busy household. That takes brains and guts, and so many skills I don't even have time to mention. Isn't it just like you to be always concerned about others. That's what I admire most about you. Don't you realize that you might need some looking after too? I want to help to do that, Clarissa, and Gerald will be our son, not just yours, and as for John, you'll be able to see him anytime you want. The doctor is stronger than we might give him credit for. Mark my words, he will be alright. We mustn't forget he has John and Mary Ambrose. And another thing, my dearest, I have moved out of my university residence. I'm going to rent one of those new flats in Bethnal Green, and there will be room enough for us three."

Clarissa could hardly believe what she was hearing. She braced herself against the tombstone for support and wept.

"It must be Massa Jesus that send you, Agustus Brown. You is such a kind man, I wish sometimes I had education, so that somebody like you could be proud of me."

"Don't cry, dear, please don't cry. I have loved you from the moment you first came into that sitting room in Chelsea, bringing us tea. Don't you realize how potent your presence is? I have wrestled with this, my dear, more than you will know. Yes, I'm supposed to be well educated, but I am more fascinated by your simplicity than anything I have ever studied. Please marry me. I'd be the happiest man in the world."

* * * * *

CHAPTER 17

Free School

D r. Meitner was not quite the same when he was discharged from the hospital. Though it was to be expected, the change in him still surprised me. There were times when I found him staring fixedly ahead for long periods. He was heavily medicated and it was difficult to wean him off the drugs. He lived in a world where he and his wife still courted, and he would call her name again and again, referring to her as "my darling." I was so moved by his devotion and innocent fidelity that I again vowed never to reveal what I knew. Every now and again he would experience complete lucidity, and it was during such a time that he set about registering Gerald and me in the Jews' Free School in Spitalfields.

There were more than seventy teachers on staff, the discipline was reputed to be first class, and their expectations and achievements were high. Many students had gone on to become professionals, and the same was expected from the rest of us.

There were hundreds of students, almost all of them Jews, and hundreds more were waiting for acceptance into the coeducational school, the largest of its kind in England. There was no mistaking that we were all from the slums. Not only was our dress similar, but there was something in every classmate's eyes that spoke of poverty, like an invisible uniform.

The teachers, too, wore layers of clothing to ward off the damp that permeated the whole school.

Gerald and I were in the same classroom with about twenty-five other boys. We were the only ones in class exempt from studying the Talmud and the Torah, though we both benefited from the school's academic competitive spirit.

We became familiar with Hebrew words and Yiddish, and saw how London Jews felt superior to new arrivals from Europe. But I will never forget the feeling of acceptance. Gerald and I never felt inferior, perhaps because it was assumed that we, too, had experienced oppression and racial intolerance. We participated in the observation of Jewish holidays and holy days. Gerald and I, even after living with the Meitners, had not been aware of Purim, Sukkot, Rosh Hashanah, Shavuoth, and Yom Kippur. But there was always Clarissa at home to remind us not to forget that we were Christian.

* * * * *

Clarissa married Mr. Brown in 1931, when Britain was still feeling the effects of the depression. Unemployment had increased throughout the country, and there was a cut in benefits for those on the dole. Mr. Brown, though, felt that things would soon be looking up since, according to him, the world was changing for the better. Women had been included in the Olympics for the first time back in 1928, and they earned the right to vote in Britain at the age of twenty-one.

"With women given more opportunity and authority, why wouldn't things get better?" he asked cheerfully, his eyes fixed firmly on Clarissa.

Their wedding was a very small affair that took place in the chapel at Saint Dunstan's. Clarissa said that at thirty-six years old, she felt old being a bride.

"Sacred Heart of Jesus!" Mary Ambrose exclaimed. "You'se not old, not you'se. Everything is so lovely, it makes me want to cry. Don't mind if I shed a wee tear do you?"

A few of their friends from the factory were in attendance, as well as a couple of Mr. Brown's associates. Clarissa wore a well-fitting second-hand navy blue suit, with a corsage of yellow roses. Her hair was attractively styled under a small veiled hat, and the smile on her dimpled cheeks was radiant. Dr. Meitner did the honour of giving her away, and Mary Ambrose, dressed in pink lace, was her only attendant. Gerald and I were proud to witness the proceedings, though we felt somewhat deserted when the happy couple left for a week in Oban, Scotland.

"John, I don't want to leave you and the doctor," Gerald said regretfully. "You're like my family now, especially since Mamma has Mr. Brown, and I wouldn't be surprised if they start a family."

I felt for Gerald, for though I knew Clarissa loved him more than life itself, and that Mr. Brown would be a caring father, I couldn't help thinking that he was right. If Clarissa started a family, there would not be enough room in the small flat for him, especially now that he was getting older. I had often heard it said that there was not enough room in one of those new flats to swing a cat.

I was sixteen years old that year and thought nothing of it when news came that Japan had invaded Manchuria in China. Only briefly did it cross my mind that Madam would have been angry about such news, but I was too concerned with my studies. I was going into sixth form, and I didn't even notice the activities in our household. Mary Ambrose had started to bring home a red-haired Irish boyfriend named Aaron Philips. He was thirty years old and worked as an overseer at the factory. To everyone but myself, it would have been obvious that they were spending far too much time in her bedroom. For even at twenty-one, Mary Ambrose was as mischievous as the day when I first met her.

CHAPTER 18

Salma's Story

By the end of the year, Dr. Meitner showed a remarkable improvement. It was as though he had taken a new lease on life. Not only did he have the repairs to the house seen to, but he also installed electric lighting and a telephone. But in spite of that, he began to spend his days and the occasional night away from home. He had plunged himself into working with refugees and seemed to have found something to sustain him because he looked healthy and robust. He worked side by side with patriotic Jews and felt useful because his services as a physician were constantly in demand.

Gerald, more often than not, was with us. We studied together, argued over schoolwork, ate, and inevitably talked about our new friendships. He was probably more sensitive to his mother's and Mr. Brown's need to spend time alone than he ever admitted.

One late November afternoon, Gerald and I were reading *Jude the Obscure* in the sitting room. Neither of us could agree whether Jude was to be admired or pitied, but we were so transported by the events in his life that all else around us was suspended. Finally, we decided to take a break after studying for hours as our brains felt ragged and tired.

Gerald and I poured hot cocoa into mugs, and there was a look of contentment on his face. His expression spoke volumes and I wondered if Gerald had come to terms with something on his mind. I looked at him expectantly, and he leaned toward me and smiled ruefully.

"John," he said, "that girl at school—I think her name is Ruth Sloan—she was looking at you. I could swear she likes you. Have you noticed her?"

To be honest, I was not even aware of Ruth Sloan's attention, if in fact there was ever any. I thought she was somewhat attractive, though her waiflike face was small and skinny, with large frightened brown eyes. Her thick brown hair had a mind of its own, and never kept itself confined to pins and bows. But considering the deplorable conditions that many Jewish refugee students were forced to live in at home, it was remarkable that she always managed to look clean.

"Gerald," I said testily, "we both know that all Ruth wants is help with her English. She's Hungarian, isn't she? Perhaps it's you she likes. I have often seen her looking over to where you sit, then quickly turning away. Wouldn't you say she's just shy?"

"Really? Do you honestly think she might like me? There's something about her John, but she's a Jew. Can you imagine how Mamma would go on and on about it if she knew?"

"Do you tell your mother everything?"

"Yes, she's always asking, so I tell her. She has even been hinting that there are some West Indians over near Limehouse. She wonders why we don't go over there. But can you honestly see me doing that, John? Not me. There are all kinds of criminals there, and gangsters too, and even more Chinese than you have ever seen. You're lucky you don't have to tell anybody anything."

"Gerald, that's not lucky. I still miss having someone."

"Don't you tell the doctor things?"

"You must be joking."

"So which girl do you like at school?"

"All of them," I answered with a grin. I couldn't bring myself to tell Gerald that two girls had already kissed me, not counting Mary Ambrose. There was Delores Goldstein, an English-born Jew who, in my second week at school, had taken me behind the blackboard on the pretence of looking for a fallen stick of chalk. Once behind the board, she groped me and planted a soggy kiss on my lips, which I managed to wriggle away from. The other was a shy withdrawn girl with soft yellow curls. She was called Lidia Karma and was from the Ukraine. The class had made a Sukkot booth from willow branches, and some of us had gone inside the enclosed structure to test its sturdiness. I found myself alone inside with Lidia. She looked at me, smiling, and I looked at her, and the next thing we knew, we were kissing. I was never alone with her again, and after that, whenever she saw me, she tended to avoid me.

In the middle of our conversation, we heard the front door key turn in the lock. We immediately stopped the conversation and armed ourselves with our schoolbooks as though deep in concentration.

It was Dr. Meitner returning home from work earlier than usual and, to our surprise, was accompanied by an attractive woman with long fair hair. She was in her early thirties, with friendly green eyes and strong, sinewy limbs.

"Good afternoon," she said, extending her hand. "I'm Salma. I'm a colleague of Dr. Meitner, though I call him Edvard. What a pleasure to meet you both at last."

There was a curious expression on her oval face as she shook our hands, and the enthusiasm in her eyes was mingled with a strange sadness. I couldn't stop looking at her. I had never met anyone with so much charisma, and I was pleased when she quickly pulled up a chair to join us.

"You are John and Gerald, correct? I've heard about you both. I work with Edvard, you see. We have a particular interest in refugees. I myself have worked in a similar capacity for years, but I am glad to find someone like Edvard, who is equally motivated. And now it seems that I am wanting help myself. The problem is my brother, Abraham. Edvard has told me that you are well aware of the horrendous persecution, harassment, and loss of dignity that has come upon our fellow Jews in Europe. He told me that you, John, have done your utmost to help our cause."

I felt Gerald's eyes on me, hot and staring, but I was too riveted by what Salma was saying and knew that even if I wanted to, I couldn't have looked away. I watched fascinated as she took out a silver cigarette case from her blazer's breast pocket, and carefully selected a cigarette, then leaned into the doctor for a light. Their movements were so synchronized that I knew it had to be something they had done often before.

Salma's jaws looked strong and her lips sensual as she pulled on the cigarette, then blew out smoke, the cigarette held firmly between two fingers.

"I am an Austrian Jew," she said, her voice husky with smoke. "I came to England ten years ago when things in Europe were not as bad as they are now. My parents sent me here to learn English and hopefully to study medicine. My father was a doctor, you see, and he wanted one of his children to follow in his footsteps. At first I had a hard time with the language and did not do well, though I qualified as a medical assistant. I have not attempted to study further because of the time it takes and the language is so overwhelming.

"In Vienna, my family was well known. My mother, Anna Heyliger, taught drama, and my father, Dr. Wolfgang Heyliger's medical practice was in the best part of the city. You might not know it, but Vienna is an old city, with so many beautiful things—baroque statues, exquisitely built opera houses, gardens, theatres, concert halls, ballrooms, and museums. The architectural styles range from Gothic to Renaissance. Parts of Vienna are much the same as London, I suppose, but there is more emphasis on the arts there.

"My father had a very busy social life, and his name was always first on the lists when invitations were sent to attend balls, teas, concerts, and operas. Our home was a little way from the city, near the river. Six servants were in our employ. Many famous musicians played in our ballroom, and artists clamoured to hang paintings on our walls. My mother, too, enjoyed notoriety. Not only was she the wife of a renowned surgeon, but she enjoyed the company of many fine actors that she taught, and she had a hand in directing major plays. But in spite of their popularity, my parents were very down to earth. They loved us and, like all other Viennese parents, wanted the best for their children—a good education, with a good command of English. That is why when my brother, Abraham, wanted to come to England, they willingly agreed. Abraham was twenty and had completed his schooling and wanted to pursue further studies, perhaps in theatre or dance. Being young, he was undecided, especially after having had experience in both disciplines.

"However, something was to happen that would change everything. One day my father went to work as usual. He was in his examination room with a patient when suddenly, some well-dressed men burst in, demanding to know if he was indeed Dr. Wolfgang Heyliger. When he said he was, the men handcuffed him and took him away. No explanations were given, and he has not been heard from since. Were it not for that patient, Helmut Cohen, we would never have known what took place.

"As you can imagine, Viennese people began to get nervous that there would be more such incidents, but they were led to believe that such incidents were isolated and the work of an underground criminal organization. None of this appeased my mother's grief and anxiety. It was obvious to her that these criminals targeted prominent Jews. She and Abraham remained in our house, avoiding all outside contact. Even the servants were let go. But as fate would have it, one day a message came, signed by our chancellor, requesting my mother's presence at the opening of a new play. It said that because of her creative work, she would be receiving one of Austria's highest medals of honour at the opening. Abraham doubted the message was genuine, and he tried to talk my mother out of attending, but she was unconvinced and was subsequently lured out of the house, only to disappear. The last I heard was that Abraham might still be alive because someone said he was seen near the German border, though I would like to believe that he could arrive at any time among the refugees coming into England. That is why I want to help to improve his odds because the sad truth is that fifty percent of the refugees who set out to cross Europe do not make it. Many people, as you already know, die during arduous wintry journeys of days without food and water. We have to increase our aid to refugees. I'm asking help from you both. We need people who can handle guns, people to act as guides, people to carry supplies, food, and blankets, and people who are willing to take risks and can think on their feet and follow directions. How about it, boys? I think our Edvard, more than any of us, needs to clear his mind before we begin. His work is stressful as it is, though he is a brilliant physician, not to mention what he has been through. But don't put away your schoolbooks on my account, boys. I came to your house because I invited Edvard to the People's Palace. It's not far from here and it will be good therapy for him. He has neglected to allow entertainment into his life, and I intend to provide that in every way I can. Edvard needs to change out of his work clothes. So tomorrow, boys, if you are interested, we can all begin training in earnest."

The People's Palace, a place of entertainment, was close to where we lived. Everyone knew it was little more than a glorified music hall, though much larger, and had more pretension than respectability. To gain entrance, one had to be in Sunday best clothing. It was particularly imposing inside, with a massive organ in its main hall. Occasionally circuses, horse and donkey shows, military tattoos, and concerts were held there. That night there was to be a concert called "Wheel Barrow of Flowers," a comedy.

It was hard for me to imagine Dr. Meitner or, for that matter,

Salma in such a setting, for the galleys were usually jam-packed with local ruffians, prostitutes, and the lower class, and both the doctor and Salma would stand out since they were "from over the bridge," as the wealthier classes from the other side of the Thames were called.

Naturally, Gerald wanted me to explain what I had been doing to help the Jewish cause. He was more than surprised to find that I had kept so much from him.

"John, you're braver than I could ever be. It must have been all the training with the puppet stage when you were younger that prepared you for all those impersonations. Come to think of it, now I know why you didn't want to talk about that printing room below stairs in the Chelsea house. I wonder if Ben Simmington was helping Mrs. Meitner with the printing."

I did not realize that after all that time, Gerald was still curious about the printing room. I still could not bring myself to reveal what the true purpose of Ben's visits to the printing room might have been.

"Gerald," I said, "it wasn't the puppetry that prepared me. It's because I once lived with a wonderful woman who was a story-teller. She had the most extraordinary way of making things come to life. I have never met anyone like her. She had a way, which is hard to explain, but it was almost as though she set me on fire with creativity. Her name was Fiona Shaw. She's American."

Gerald looked incredulous as he jokingly snatched my book away from me.

"You don't need this," he said. "Your life could fill a volume."

We laughed and I wanted to tell him about Madam and my speaking Hakka, but I decided to save it for another occasion.

I had not thought about Madam or Miss Shaw for the longest time, and the memory of them brought tears. It was well after ten in the evening before Dr. Meitner returned home. Gerald and I heard excited voices in the hallway. One voice was somewhat familiar. At first I thought perhaps it might be Mary Ambrose, but

147

since she was spending the evening at Aaron Philips's, I knew it wasn't her. Then I heard the person say my name and Gerald's, and it was as though something from my past had come back to haunt me. I could not imagine who it could be, and I had to restrain myself from bursting into the hall to see for myself. Gerald must have felt the same way, for he was already about to get up when a smiling Dr. Meitner and Salma entered the sitting room with Mercedes Williams alongside them.

"Look who we found performing at the People's Palace," Dr. Meitner announced. "You remember her, don't you?"

"Auntie!" I exclaimed, surprised that I remembered the name she had asked me to call her.

"Who's this?" Mercedes asked, looking at me and then throwing her head back with laughter. "This couldn't be the little boy who came over on the banana boat, could it? This is a young man, and a handsome one at that! And don't tell me that that big good-looking man over there is Gerald! Where has the time gone?"

Gerald stood up to his full height and shook her hand.

"Hello, Miss Williams. What a pleasure."

Mercedes smiled broadly.

"Gerald, you sound like an Englishman. What a difference time can make. How's your mother?"

"Clarissa married an American professor," I said, interrupting Gerald before he had any chance to downplay his mother's circumstance. "He was our tutor actually, but we weren't his only students."

"Clarissa's married! Oh my stars, how wonderful for her! I have been back and forth to Jamaica myself, and missed out on a lot of what was happening here. I was so sorry to hear about what happened to Mrs. Meitner. She was such a striking-looking woman. It's hard to forget her. So, are you boys still in school?"

"Yes, ma'am," Gerald replied. "We're at the Jew's Free School, and we rather like it."

"It's a good school," said Mercedes, holding my hand firmly in her soft one. "It has a good reputation all over England because those Jews, they know about education. Consider yourselves lucky."

* * * * *

We had a quick glass of white wine together before Salma announced that she had an early start in the morning.

"It was a pleasure meeting you, Miss Williams," she said huskily. "Edvard is driving me home. I hope we can meet again soon. Good night, boys. Let's talk tomorrow."

Dr. Meitner was immediately on his feet. It was obvious that he was attracted to Salma, for there was no mistaking the adoration in his eyes.

"Don't wait up for me. It was a pleasure, Mercedes. Why don't you stay and visit with the boys? If it gets late, there's Mary Ambrose's room. There's still a spare bed in there."

The moment the couple left, Mercedes Williams drew her chair up even closer. She didn't look even a day older than when I had last seen her. She was just as vivacious, and she had a wonderful spark of life running through her.

"So this is where you're living now," she said, looking around at the attractive furnishings in the room. "You've all done a good job here. What a comfortable home."

"You should have seen where we were before," Gerald said. "It had rooms galore and a huge garden. It was almost like a palace."

"Well, the doctor must have had a good reason for giving it all up because many of the things you have here in this room are worth more than the house itself. I wonder if he lives here just because he wants to be close to other Jews and to experience first-hand the environment they live in. I'm sure you've noticed that a lot of the Jews around here are refugees. Whatever his reason, it's good to see that he hasn't deserted you both. He has been quite responsible, wouldn't you say?"

149

"I suspect he's starting to care for Salma too," I said. "I haven't seen him look this contented in years."

"Do you boys know who Salma Heyliger is?"

"Yes, ma'am," Gerald replied, "she works with the doctor at a refugee clinic here in East End London."

"Not that," Mercedes said smugly. "There are things you probably wouldn't know about her, but she is famous in the Jewish underground community. If it wasn't for the fact that I'm in the theatre world with contacts with other actors, I would never have met people who even knew her famous mother. Gypsies and Jews in the theatres from Europe all speak with hushed voices about Salma, who they all say led them through the mountains to escape intolerance, which is festering in Europe. To them, it is as though she is a deity, for she has helped so many. Some call her the White Angel. She was married briefly to a man they referred to as the Ferry Man. He was responsible for conveying many refugees to both England and Sweden in his boat. His name was Tobias Gabin. She never speaks about him, and it is said that he disappeared on a mission. I wouldn't doubt that the doctor is involved with Salma's cause. Anyway, boys, much as I would like to chat, it's getting late, so let's see about bed, shall we?"

CHAPTER 19

Limehouse

The next morning, Mercedes Williams was up as early as I was. I went into the kitchen to decide what to prepare for breakfast. There were a few eggs and a bottle of milk, as well as pickled fish and leftover cabbage rolls in the refrigerator. There was little more than a scrap of flour in a tin, as well as a jar with cornmeal. I was puzzling over what to do with what little there was when I saw Mercedes at the kitchen door.

"Good morning, you're up early," she said. "Need help?"

I nodded in response and laid out my selections—flour, cornmeal, and eggs—on the table and then filled the kettle.

"Well, besides cocoa," I said, "I wasn't sure what to make for all of us."

"Since it is just you, me, and Gerald, you don't need to make much because I eat like a bird."

"What about Dr. Meitner?"

"He didn't come home, John. I'm a light sleeper and I would have heard him."

"In that case, how does fried cornmeal dumplings and eggs sound?"

"It sounds fine. John, I'm so proud to see how you can handle yourself in this country. I hope you will find someone worthy of you. If only I was forty-something years younger."

We both laughed. It felt so natural being with Mercedes in the early hours.

"Where do you live, Auntie?"

"Bloomsbury. There are lots of writers and creative people there, much the same as in Chelsea, I suppose. I also rent a flat in Limehouse. I often perform over there, so it saves on my travelling back and forth."

"I've never been to Limehouse, though it's close, but I have heard it is not safe."

"Don't believe everything you hear, John. It's true that there is a lot of criminal activity, but it's not all bad. In fact, I do free shows there for the children. Those children hardly have anything, they are so poor. You should see them. Some even walk barefoot and wear rags much like the poor back in Jamaica. It is strange, John, but many people back home seem to think that all White people are rich. If only they could see these children. Every day or so, around two in the afternoon, I set up a little booth near the wharf, and all the seamens' children, the street urchins, the Chinese fresh off the boat, and many others, such as the black-skinned children of Africans and a few West Indians, come to watch me make monkey faces and dance like an idiot. I even sing some old songs like 'Peel Neck John Crow,' and you should hear how they all laugh."

"I'd love to see you, Auntie."

"Well, how about coming with me tomorrow because it's Saturday? Bring Gerald. Now, let me give you a hand with those dumplings. You can fry the eggs."

"Auntie," I said hesitantly, "would you like to have a puppet stage for the children?"

"Would I like one, John? I would love one. Have you got one to give?"

"Yes, I do."

*****

Dr. Meitner did not return home that morning, and though

152

Gerald and I waited expectantly for him, or even Salma, neither of them showed up. It wasn't the first time that he had stayed out all night, and we felt there was no cause for concern.

"If I were alone with someone like Salma," I said jokingly, "I'd be away all night too."

That evening over baked beans and toast, I told Gerald about Mercedes's invitation to Limehouse, and was surprised when he readily agreed to accompany me. But then he told me that Ruth Sloan's family lived near there, and I realized why he'd had a change of heart about the area.

"Who knows? I might get to see her," he said. "She even talked to me today, she told me that she is learning English quickly, but her family, Orthodox Jews, are reluctant to learn. She wanted to know where I was from, and said she used to live near Budapest. They were as poor there as they are here, but her grandmother, who's supposed to be a reader of the Kabbala, predicted that many bad things would happen to them if they remained there. So her father, a pastry maker, packed up everything, bought an old lame horse and a wagon with what little they had, and left the country. She and her parents, her grandmother, and her younger sister, Irene, travelled for weeks, taking turns walking alongside the horse-drawn wagon. She said they met hostility everywhere they went, though when they pretended to be fortune-telling gypsies, they were given food and sometimes shelter in Czechoslovakia. Then when they got to Poland, they traded the horse and wagon for a boat trip to Denmark, and from there they made their way to England."

"Gerald, it sounds like the more you know about Ruth, the more you like her."

"Who said anything about 'like'? I love the girl, John."

"Well, you know exactly what your mother will say, Gerald, and I don't mean about her being a Jew, but about your studies. She'll say, 'Let nothing come between you and your schoolwork.' Won't she?"

"Believe me, John, Ruth won't come between me and anything. In fact, she makes me want to make something of myself. That's why I'm aiming high. Scholarship time is coming up, and I intend to be among those who succeed."

* * * * *

Mercedes Williams's entertainment booth, made from a collapsible bamboo frame and decorated with crepe paper, was set up near the West India docklands inside a Commercial Road warehouse. I had never seen her so animated. She painted her face garishly, and put on a long pointed cap like a jester's. She wore a floppy clown suit, and had bells jingling at her ankles. She had a huge trunk of costumes at her disposal. She handed me a pirate's hat and Gerald a bongo drum and an eye patch, then winked at us both.

"Play the drum, Gerald," she said laughing. "Play any tune, even make something up. The children will come, for the sound of the bongo is the signal that the show is on."

And come they did. There were ragged children everywhere, their dirt-smudged faces beaming, their toes tapping, as Mercedes played on a tambourine and danced.

Remembering the puppet stage we brought, I whispered, "Could I please do a very short puppet show?" I was so carried away by the excitement that I wanted more than anything to be part of it, and I hoped Mercedes wouldn't mind.

And she didn't mind. "Why certainly. I'd love to see you perform."

We placed the stage atop three old crates so that I could stand behind them without being seen. I decided to perform Red Riding Hood because it was so well known, and then, on the spur of the moment, decided to have the wolf speak in Hakka. How the children roared with laughter! Afterwards, a whole tribe of Chinese children followed me, as though I were the Piper of Hamlin.

"Where did you learn to speak Chinese?" Gerald asked with a grin. "What else don't I know about you, John?"

I went over to watch Gerald as he played happily on the bongo, and briefly whispered to him.

"Another wonderful woman that I lived with taught me Hakka."

Gerald smiled broadly, and looked at me with a mixture of disbelief and admiration.

"She was my guardian, Madam Hung Chin," I said, and I touched him lightly on his shoulder to reassure him and smiled.

"No more surprises," I said. "There are many Chinese dialects. A lot of these children speak Cantonese and Mandarin. Isn't it interesting that so many of them recognize Hakka?"

CHAPTER 20

Changing Times

On Sundays, Mr. Brown and Clarissa often dropped by to take Gerald and me for a drive around London. Sometimes, if Mary Ambrose was not occupied with her love life, she too would accompany us. I imagined that those drives were not merely for sightseeing, but were well thought-out social studies projects so that we could see history for ourselves—the ancient monuments, churches, and other interesting architectural structures.

We became acutely aware that London, like Kingston, had a dark underbelly, though Mr. Brown was quick to point out that much was being done to change things, for there were almshouses, hospitals, and vigilant policing, as well as an army. He said that the Jews, though despised at first, had brought with them a thirst for knowledge, and the Chinese had shown passive tolerance in the face of opposition, which surely had an effect on those around them. It was the Irish, he said, who would not stand for being treated badly. Mr. Brown also pointed out that there were very few West Indians in London, and the few that were there had resigned themselves into blending in with the British, so they had no real identity. But that, he said, could change dramatically if their numbers increased.

* * * * *

When Mr. Brown and Clarissa arrived that Sunday afternoon to collect us, Gerald and I were already waiting anxiously. The doctor had still not returned home, so we were somewhat anxious. Clarissa's knock at the door caused us both to jump to our feet, and when we let her and Mr. Brown in, they seemed to brim with excitement. Clarissa's cheeks were flushed and pink, and Mr. Brown, who had begun to wear a hat, threw it in the air with abandon.

"I've brought a bottle of Spanish wine. Crack out the glasses. Where's everyone?"

"Dr. Meitner is away," I said hesitantly, "but Mary Ambrose is in her room."

"Then call her! This is indeed a special occasion."

Gerald bounded up the stairs, and in no time, Mary Ambrose came behind him. She looked pale, wan, and overworked.

"Oh God Almighty! T'is you," she said, brightening up the moment she saw Clarissa. "I'se been sleeping so soundly. But not to worry, luv, what's this ruckus all about?"

Clarissa handed her a glass of wine and the rest of us stood around with our glasses, hardly daring to breathe.

"I'm four months pregnant," Clarissa said, gently patting her stomach. "The doctors think it might be twins."

I will never forget the look on Gerald's face. First his eyes were wide with amazement, then they softened, and the tears that stained his cheeks were pure joy.

Mary Ambrose wept too and hid her swollen eyes behind her hair.

"God and his holy mother! And you'se not said a word all these months, Clarissa. You'se must think I'm a right pain that would go blabbing it about."

"Is not that," Clarissa said laughing. "Is just that ... we wanted to be quite sure before we say anything, and then things go spoil. But now that Dr. Edmonds say that all is well, I tell Agustus is time we say something."

* * * * *

Dr. Meitner returned home late that night. He immediately went into the kitchen and washed his hands.

"It's been a trying weekend," he said. "There has been an outbreak of fevers, and I'm sad to say we lost three of our patients. To make matters worse, Salma received word that her brother has been detained in Germany. She is devastated. She is in such a state that I don't think she will be doing any training for a while, but I will help her in every way that I can. I intend to marry her, you see."

* * * * *

I was eighteen years old in 1933 when I received a scholarship to the London School of Journalism, a faculty of the University of London. It was a double celebration, for Gerald had also earned a scholarship and would be attending the London School of Economics. How amused we were to think that when we were sixteen, we had thought ourselves ready for scholarships and the disciplined life of university. Little did we realize then that it would take a tough uphill battle to achieve our goals. In the end, the entire staff at the Jews' Free School was proud of us. Mr. Kudelski, our form room teacher; Miss Silverstein, the math teacher, and even Mr. Isaacs, who guided us through geography, all admitted that when we first arrived at the school, they were not sure what to expect, but when they discovered that Mr. Brown had been our tutor, they had no longer had any doubts about our eventual success.

A celebratory dinner was held in honour of the school's successful scholarship recipients. Families and friends were invited, and the dining room was filled to capacity. Mr. Brown, Dr. Meitner, Mercedes Williams, Salma, and Mary Ambrose were all there.

"You did well, Gerald," said Ruth Sloan, joining us at our table. "You too, John. I wish I could have worked as hard. Congratulations!"

"Come over here," Gerald said boldly. "Do you call graduating with top marks not doing well? I remember when you didn't even speak English. Look how quickly you learned. What are your plans for the future?"

"Well, I thought about medicine, but I don't know how I'd deal with death on a daily basis, so I'll probably go into law. That way I can have a hand in improving things for other refugees. But when I think about how far I have come since leaving Hungary, it amazes me. I'm glad I had this opportunity."

"Me too," I said. "Imagine—just a few years ago, I didn't even know a thing about England."

"Ever think of going back to Jamaica?"

"Who, me?"

"Yes, you, John. I know I'll never return to Hungary. My heart is no longer there."

"Yes, I think I'd like to go back to Jamaica. I think about it often, as a matter of fact. How about you, Gerald?"

"I agree, John, and considering that we were children when we came here, we had no say in the matter. I think now that I can make my own decisions, I'd like to return."

"Well, I suppose this is it then," Ruth said softly, her eyes heavy with regret. "I'll probably never see either of you again. Whatever you end up doing in your lives, good luck."

Ruth nodded to the others at the table and was about to take her leave. She held her slim back straight, and her long hair cascaded almost as far as her waist. She had blossomed like a flower—there was colour in her cheeks, and one could not help noticing how particularly attractive she looked in her burgundy strapless dress.

Gerald must have experienced a moment's panic, for it seemed that the thing he had dreaded for the last couple of years had come to pass—Ruth was going out of his life. He frantically fumbled in his breast pocket, then quickly reached out and grabbed her by the wrist.

"This is for you, Ruth," he said shyly, oblivious to everyone else at the table. "I have been saving it for the right occasion, and now I see there might never be another occasion." He smiled nervously and slipped a small gold ring into Ruth's palm. "This was my grandmother's ring. I vowed that it would always remain in our family. So I'm taking a big risk in giving it to you, Ruth, but it is with the hope that it will stay in the family."

I was stunned by Gerald's boldness, though thrilled by the theatrics of his proposal. What would Clarissa say? And how would Ruth's parents and Mr. Brown react if Ruth accepted it?

Ruth Sloan laughed softly, and rubbed her thumb over the ring.

"This is so lovely, Gerald, but I'm sorry, I can't accept it." She added quickly, "I think that getting engaged now would hold you back. I hope you're not offended because it would be such an honour if you'll ask me to wear it when you've finished your studies. Meanwhile, I'd like you to meet my family."

None of us at the table knew what to say. I had never thought about marriage myself, and assumed that Gerald had felt the same way. Mr. Brown cleared his throat noisily, a curious expression on his face, then reached over to nudge Gerald.

"Go," he said encouragingly. "The girl wants you to meet her family."

Mary Ambrose who had been unusually quiet throughout the exchange, smiled broadly, mischief in her eyes. "Jesus mercy!" she said, "I'se dead happy. Didn't know he had it in him, did I. T'is good to see the lad's got balls."

* * * * *

Clarissa, who had given birth to twins Rupert Agustus and Mary Clarissa, was unable to attend the event. The twins were a year old and fidgety. How proud of them we all were.

Mary Ambrose in particular took a special interest. She had not married, and after her Irish boyfriend, Aaron Philips, returned to Dublin, she underwent an illegal abortion, performed by a so-called "midwife" on Rose Mary Lane. Mary Ambrose claimed that it would not have been possible for her to raise a child alone, but although she survived the trauma of the brutal surgery, she was never again able to conceive.

As appropriate to my first year in university, Dr. Meitner saw to it that I was always well dressed and presentable. He said it was his way of preparing me for the future when I would need to look the part and meet the right sort of people.

"It's fashionable to wear a hat these days," he said. "Make sure you have one in your wardrobe, and don't forget to wear a good tie."

It was probably because of my fine clothing that so many women found me interesting and attractive. As a result, I almost always had a young woman on my arm, though I had no thoughts of settling down. To me, unlike Gerald, all that sort of thing seemed far in the future.

Despite the increasing demands of my studies, I somehow still managed to find time on Saturdays to accompany Mercedes Williams to the Limehouse slums to perform at her free shows. But as time went on, she grew frail and I was obliged to offer her more and more assistance, which I enjoyed. The adrenaline from the performances was equal to the excitement of having opportunities to practise speaking my Hakka, which was a link with my past with Madam.

Though Dr. Meitner never remarried, he and Salma occasionally lived as a couple in their separate homes. I wondered if the arrangement had anything to do with the possibility that Salma's husband might still be alive. But a greater cause for their concern was a charismatic new leader, also an Austrian, had had a meteoric rise to power in Germany. His name was Adolph Hitler. As chancellor, Adolph Hitler was restraining his openly anti-Semitic opinions, which were that Aryans were the master race, and that all other races were inferior. Salma's brother's welfare weighed heavily on her mind because as far as she was concerned, he could not have found himself in a more dangerous place. As she had anticipated, ominous news arrived from Europe. Germany withdrew from the League of Nations. Hitler would agree to world peace only if all the other nations were willing to recognize its equality, but there was no indication that other nations were about to do so.

Mr. Brown, who on a drizzly morning was walking the twins, stopped in at a newsagent and learned that not only did a Coloured American, Jesse Owens, prove Hitler's race theory wrong by winning gold medals at the German Olympics, but that Albert Einstein, a Jew and the most brilliant scientific mind of our time, had decided to leave Germany to take up residence in the United States.

CHAPTER 21

Elizabeth

Georg V, our King, celebrated his Silver Jubilee in May 1935, and all of London was caught up in the excitement. Streets were decorated and Union Jacks were on display everywhere. Public houses overflowed with citizens wishing the King well, and even the poor felt the surge of enthusiasm, for they, too, benefited from the sudden generosity of the other celebrants. The King was much admired for having a common touch, and his annual Christmas message to his subjects made him ever dearer to them.

I was twenty years old that year. Mercedes Williams must have been almost eighty, but she insisted that the children of the poor should not be forgotten in the excitement. Music halls were closed down and replaced with cinemas. And although boxing was popular, it, too, was a paying event. Some residents flocked to the notorious gambling dens in Whitechapel, which ate up their wages in short order. Nothing was free, especially for children, so it took little persuasion on Mercedes's part to have me agree to assist with her performance. Mr. Brown was kind enough to drive us and our equipment over to Limehouse. "There's more bad news from Europe," Mr. Brown said, his eyes downcast. "You already know that the Austrian chancellor, Engelbert Dollfuss, was killed by Nazis two years ago. Well, as if that wasn't bad enough, there are rumours that the Jews in Germany are going to be deprived of all their civil rights. It can't help but remind me of the Jim Crow laws in the United States against Negroes. I personally think that England will become involved sooner or later because I don't see us standing by and doing nothing to help if that comes to pass."

"Let's just enjoy this day, for what it is," Mercedes said softly. "It could well be my last performance."

*****

When we arrived at the old warehouse, there were ragged children everywhere. Some had even climbed up on top of the highest crates, while others squatted on the floor. There was tumultuous applause when the booth was set up, and some of the children blew on cheap whistles. If I had not already guessed at Mercedes's age I would have thought she was a much younger woman, for that day she demonstrated the agility and form of an athletic dancing clown, much to the amusement of all. That day, because of the tremendous turnout, I decided to perform two puppet shows, and as usual I had one of the characters speaking in Hakka. How wonderful it was to hear the room erupt with laughter and generous applause.

After the performances, children gathered around as usual. Among them was a sad-eyed, blondish little boy of about four years old. He hung onto the legs of my trousers and would not let go. I sat on a crate and helped to pack away our equipment, but still the boy held on. He looked me full in the face, and my heart almost stopped, he was so beautiful, and I saw that his blue eyes had that wonderful fold in the lid particular to Orientals, and I knew he was Eurasian.

"What's your name, little guy?" I said smiling, even as I felt his grip tighten.

"I'm Charlie."

"I'm John," I said. "Are you here alone?" I looked around the room, but because so many people still milled around, it was impossible to tell who belonged with whom.

"Where's Mummy?" I asked, looking in the direction of the crowd, who had come to enjoy free tea and sandwiches as well as the entertainment.

"Is he lost?" Mercedes asked, coming to join us. She patted the child affectionately on his head. "What a dear child," she said, "and look, John, his hair is almost as fair as yours."

"Mummy over there," Charlie said, giving me a tug and pointing to the back of the room. I took his small hand in mine. How warm and reassuring it felt. Together we walked across the creaking floors, past where booths had been set up serving tea and small sandwiches. There was a whiff of industry in the air from the nearby factories, and the cooing sounds of pigeons was almost music-like in the decaying rafters above. All around us I heard the murmur of conversations about the King's Jubilee, and how splendid it would be.

I felt elated, almost buoyant, and so caught up with the festivities that at first I didn't see Charlie's mother. Then suddenly there she was, with her back turned toward us. A swish of long, straight hair cascaded over her slim shoulders. She was taller than I expected, and was wearing a simple brown dress with short sleeves.

"Mamma!" Charlie cried out loudly. "I bring puppet man!"

She turned round quickly, and I saw that she was Oriental. And her hair, her wonderful hair, seemed to float as she turned. I had never seen a face like hers. How luminous it was, and how perfectly like almonds her brown eyes were, and her lips were like soft roses.

"You found Charlie," she said, smiling. Her low, unaccented voice sounded slightly English.

"Thanks, for bringing him back. He's always exploring by himself. I can't seem to stop him."

"He found me." I smiled back. "My name is John."

165

"Yes, I know. I saw your show. It was very good, you know. My name's Elizabeth, but where on earth did you learn to speak Hakka so well?"

"It's a long story really, but I grew up in Jamaica."

"You did?"

"Yes, my guardian was a Hakka woman, and I went to a Chinese school!"

"Isn't that extraordinary!" she said, her eyes wide. "You don't mean Miss Wang's school do you!"

"The very one," I said, noticing that her lips began to tremble.

"I'm Elizabeth Lyn. I wonder if you remember me. I was in Miss Wang's class, too. And you know what? It has just dawned on me—oh my goodness! You must be John Moneague! I never forgot your name because it is so unusual."

I was so overwhelmed that I threw my arms around her. I felt her body tremble and the butterfly wing-like beating of her heart, and I could scarcely even catch my breath.

"I always meant to go back to the school to visit," I said, "but I left the island so suddenly that there wasn't time. What has become of Miss Wang and the school?"

"We always hoped you would come back, John, but no one knew what had happened to you. As for Miss Wang, she married an ugly old toad who came from China, but last I heard, she's happy."

"What about Miss Shaw? Is she in Jamaica?"

"I don't know where she is, John. I heard her father died, and she might have gone home. I don't really know because I myself have been away for more than ten years. But how about you? Have you been living in London all this time?"

I could not let her see how deflated I was since there was no news of Miss Shaw. I reached down and hoisted Charlie up onto my shoulders, and passed a sandwich to him from one of the booths.

"I'm at the university," I said quickly. "I've been here since I left Jamaica. First I lived in Chelsea, and now in Stepney."

"You were always clever, John. Are you studying drama? I would have been too shy to perform the way you did, though I am perhaps a couple of years older than you are."

"I'm studying journalism. You're right, though. I rather enjoy acting. It's thanks to Miss Shaw, I'm sure. Anyway, tell me about yourself."

"I'm not that interesting. In fact, my life is as dull as Limehouse."

"Elizabeth, Limehouse is anything but dull. Please tell me about yourself. I'm rather interested."

"Well, I married an English soldier named Brandon Andrews back in Jamaica when I was eighteen. He was thirty, and my parents weren't keen on the idea. Then I studied under a local potter, and was just beginning to get things going. But my father passed away suddenly, and my mother was never quite the same. She went back to China and left me behind, so when Brandon sent for me to come to England, I came happily, thinking things were going to be better for me. But when I got here, I couldn't believe the conditions he lived in. I also found that he was a heavy drinker and a scoundrel, who thought nothing of using me as his live-in maid while he carried on with his womanizing. Charlie and I live in a flat near these docks."

"So what became of your husband?"

"He's still in the army. Charlie hardly ever sees him. Whenever he comes here, he is always involved in some sort of brawl. He's stationed in Manchester."

"So how do you manage?"

"I'm trying to get back into pottery because it's something I can do at home, you know, with Charlie still little and all. I'm trying to make enough ceramic pieces to be able to have a show, but I end up having to sell them. Perhaps one day I'll make enough money to take Charlie home. John, I really shouldn't be telling you all this. The last thing I want is for you to feel sorry for me."

"Feel sorry for you? No, Elizabeth, I admire you, and don't you ever feel that you can't tell me things. It is so important to share one's thoughts and dreams. I'm actually quite pleased that you have been this frank with me."

I cannot explain how I felt on seeing Elizabeth. She was strong, admirable, and determined, but then there was her husband to consider. I told myself that I would avoid seeing her again because she had opened up so many wounds from my past. Seeing her brought back longing for my beloved Madam Hung Chin, as well as wonderful memories of Miss Shaw. But in spite of my good intentions, I did not know if I could be strong enough to keep such a promise.

* * * * *

Mercedes Williams passed away in October of that year. She had made a large container of pumpkin soup and a pie for the Limehouse children before giving in to exhaustion. She lay down on her couch and remained there for two full days before gathering enough strength to call us on her phone, asking Gerald and me to come to Bloomsbury. The frailty in her voice startled us both, and we wasted no time in getting to her side. She was not alone, for when we arrived, her lawyer, Jules Maxwell, was there, a considerate, young, approachable man, who held her hand as if she were his own mother.

"John," she said huskily on seeing us, "come sit beside me. You too, Gerald. Don't be afraid of an old dying woman who loves you. I am ninety-four years old. You didn't know that, did you? I've had a wonderful run, haven't I? Last night my uncle, Horace Valentine, who has been dead for years, came to see me. Yes, I know, I know, but I saw him with my own two eyes and he told me that it's time I came to join him, and I agreed.

"Don't say a word, John. Let me speak. You've been like a grandson. And Gerald, you made an old woman happy to see how far you've come. I love both of you, and want to make things easier for you, and since I have no one else, I'm leaving everything I have to the two of you. You never knew it, my dear ones, but I'm worth over sixty thousand pounds. I was the one always providing the free tea and sandwiches. Mr. Maxwell will take care of everything. Promise you'll dance at my funeral because I wish I could be there to dance with you."

* * * * *

The month before Mercedes's death, Hitler had enforced the Nuremberg Law. As Mr. Brown had said, it systematically deprived all German Jews of their civil rights, placing every Jew on the continent in imminent danger. Mercedes had paid no attention to these developments, but in October, after she passed away, East End London was to experience a wake-up call regarding the Fascists in Europe. An organization called the British Union of Fascists staged a march there, with almost two thousand black-shirted participants. Their progress through the streets was successfully blocked by the temporary barricade of an overturned lorry and the load of bricks it had been carrying. The confrontation, which ensued with the removal of the barricade, was referred to as the Battle of Cable Street.

The day of Mercedes's funeral was the same day that the Jewish People's Council against Fascism, the Communist Party, local workers for the Labour Party, and the International Labour Defence celebrated victory over the "Blackshirts."

A memorial for Mercedes was held in the warehouse where she usually performed. There was a standing room-only audience. Every East End child came; some brought flowers, some brought their favourite toys, and, as she had requested, there was a dance.

We had intended to play gramophone records, but a small band

169

materialized from the gathering. There was a horn, a flute, a guitar, and an accordion player. Mercedes would have loved it. They struck up a waltz, and to my surprise, Charlie, from out of nowhere, found me. I picked him up and gently placed him on top of my new shoes, and waltzed him around the room. And what a rush of memories it brought.

*****

The crisis in Europe worsened in 1936. Germany invaded the Rhineland, and civil war broke out in Spain. In England, the British throne was in jeopardy. Our beloved King Edward V died earlier in the year. On his passing, the Queen wrote in her diary: "Am heartbroken. At five to twelve my darling husband passed away." Her heartbreak was echoed throughout the whole nation with the observation of national mourning. The King's eldest son, Edward, was heir to the throne, though it was revealed that he had fallen in love with a divorced American woman named Wallis Simpson. When Parliament decreed that a King could not be allowed to marry such a notorious woman, I couldn't help but empathize with him.

I myself had similar feelings for Elizabeth Lyn, which could not be described as anything else but love. I kept my word, though. I did not go out of my way to see her or maintain any contact with her, but there was no escaping her in my every thought.

While I was in that frame of mind, I began to collaborate with a fellow journalist, Faith Gayle, from the university, and together we wrote an article for *The Standard* about London's poor and its refugees. Our article appeared on page two and, to my utmost satisfaction, I earned my first byline. Faith and I searched out the most desperate and told their stories, which held London riveted on publication.

Therefore, it was not unusual to find Faith and me poring over notes in our kitchen on Mile End Road. She had become such a fixture that it was assumed that we were lovers. I was twenty-one years old and considered a man, though I saw the relationship as strictly business and platonic.

The kitchen was where Gerald found us late one evening, alone in the house. Dr. Meitner was away. In late middle age, he still worked tirelessly for his cause, which resulted in frequent clandestine travel to Europe with Salma, returning a few days later, accompanied by a new group of refugees.

Mary Ambrose had taken up daily attendance at Mass with a passion, and had gone to choir practice. It was unbelievable the change in her—the serenity and prayerfulness. If I did not know that she was seeing the son of the choirmaster, a Stephen Richards, I would have thought that she had had a divine visitation.

The kitchen was warm, comfortable, and tidy. Faith and I had our supper earlier, and were sitting with heads together when Gerald walked in unexpectedly with Ruth. He went over to the tap and washed his hands, then nodded at us both.

"Glad to see you're up, John. Ruth and I have something to say."

My heart pounded, I put my pen aside and cradled my chin in my hands, expecting the worst. Faith stood up suddenly and came to stand behind me, her hands resting on my shoulders.

"Ruth and I were married today," Gerald said nervously. "I couldn't tell anyone, I am afraid. I wasn't sure how both families would react, but the important thing is that Ruth and I are sure of each other."

I felt my legs wobble as I stood up to congratulate them. I wondered if I had lost a brother or a friend, but when Gerald and I held each other in a hearty hug, I knew I had not lost anyone.

"Congratulations," I said, hugging Ruth, realizing that she was on her honeymoon. "Faith and I are finished here." I began to clear away our piles of paper.

"Don't do that, John. We won't be staying here. Ruth and I are booked for a week's stay in a hotel in Holland Park. Maybe you and Faith will be next."

I had almost forgotten Faith. How cruel I felt, realizing that others saw us as a couple when I had no such feeling for her. I looked away, hoping that she would not read anything in my eyes. To me, she was a brilliant journalist, not my potential life partner. Her grey eyes looked crestfallen when she finally met my gaze, and she ran her thin fingers through her hair, nervously awaiting my response.

"I'll probably never marry," I said.

* * * * *

I was alone in the sitting room nearing midnight when Mary Ambrose let herself in. I could hear her giggling and thought she had brought home a friend.

"S'cuse me," she said mischievously, coming to join me on the sofa, "I had a wee drop of brandy, not to mention a drop of gin. You'se alone, John?"

"Yes, and Gerald's gone and got married. He came to tell us tonight."

"Holy Mother of God! So he's gone and done it now. Clarissa's going to hit the roof now, you know."

"That's bad enough, but now he's hinting that I might marry Faith."

"You'se a poor fellow. Do you care for Faith at all then?"

"No, but I'd hate to hurt her feelings, Mary. I'm in love with someone else."

"God Almighty! Don't go telling me it's me then. I'd be dead shocked now, 'cause you'se like me brother and all now."

"No, Mary, it's not you. It's a girl I knew years ago."

"What a dark horse! You'se never mentioned such a girl, have you now?"

"I met her again recently. She's like a dream come back to haunt me. But the worst part, Mary, is that she's married."

172

"God and his holy mother! Well someone would best be telling Faith not to be getting them ideas in her head then."

"I have never at any time given her any hope, Mary."

"Jesus, Mary! Do you mean to say you'se never even kissed her then?"

"No, Mary."

Mary Ambrose giggled mischievously.

"At least I've kissed you, John, and what a right smack it was. Someone better set Faith straight then. No use you'se wasting her time, is it? While you'se go mooning over someone else and all."

"Mary."

"Yes, John?"

"The woman I told you about, she has a son."

"God Almighty, John! Is he yours then?"

"No, Mary, but I love him, too."

CHAPTER 22

The Green Nude

*I*n 1938, Dr. Meitner made another trip to Europe with Salma, but it was almost six months before we received word regarding his whereabouts. Mary Ambrose and I had been running the house alone. I was doing the cooking and she the cleaning, but, feigning dissatisfaction with the arrangement, Mary Ambrose began to talk about leaving London to settle in Australia.

"It's a better life there, I'm sure," she said. "What's to stop me getting a piece of land and a house of me own, for little or nothing?"

"And who's going to be helping you rough it out in the outback, Mary? I can't see you living alone, with no one to give a hand."

"God Almighty! The trouble with you'se, John, is too much thinking. Maybe someone's waiting out there in them bushes for me. How am I to know, if I don't go looking then?"

She brushed past me and went out on to the front steps to put a potted flowering plant by the doorway.

"Christ!" she grumbled, "You can never put a bloody thing out here before it's gone missing."

"Don't put anything out there then," I retorted, as I bent over my latest research. It concerned a Belgian boy named Voytek Janni whose mother, Danuta, a seamstress from Bruges, and his father, Peder, a leather worker from Tongres, had successfully made it out of Belgium, by way of the underground, to freedom. According to my information, Voytek was currently living in London and was said to have a wealth of information regarding the escalating persecution of European Jews.

I was so absorbed with studying the information that I didn't hear the door. Mary Ambrose went to answer it, cursing under her breath.

"John!" she called out. "Someone's here for you'se."

I looked up to see a bearded man in a seaman's cap. His beard was as black as midnight, and his skin quite sallow.

"Have a seat." I said, stuffing my notes into a folder. The man hesitated before pulling up a chair.

"I've just put the kettle on. How about a drop of tea?"

The man didn't answer. He seemed intent on whatever it was he had come about, and he could hardly wait for Mary to leave us alone in the kitchen.

"You John Moneague?" he asked the moment Mary Ambrose left. "You the one that writes 'bout Jews and refugees?"

"Yes."

"Just wanting to be sure, sir," the man said, removing his cap and extracting a folded piece of paper from underneath the lining. "This is for you, sir. It came last night."

"What is it?"

"It's from the doctor, lad."

I quickly took the note and unfolded it carefully, then eagerly read its contents:

John,
This is written in a hurry. I'm not sure that Salma and I can make it back. Things did not go well on this mission. We stumbled upon a German patrol and have been taken prisoners. I bribed a guard to take this note out for us. By strange coincidence, he knew Salma's brother, Abraham. He

told us that Abraham survived, only because a commandant found out that he was a dancer, and required his services as an entertainer for his troops to keep their spirits up. Abraham was virtually a prisoner in the commandant's house, but somehow he got secretly involved with a radio operator who also lived in the house. They had a child together. It is said that the child's name is David. The commandant has since retired, and Abraham and all the adult Jews in the household were put on death trains. The same fate awaits me and my dearest Salma. We have heard that other arrangements were made for the children in the commandant's household, but we do not at this time know what they are.

My beloved son John, I have left instructions with my new lawyer in the event that something like this would happen. He came highly recommended by Mercedes Williams. Trust him. Please know that you are always in my thoughts. I am so very proud of you. Please forgive Sarah.

> Your loving father,
> Edvard Meitner

Yes, I thought, after pondering over his words. I have forgiven Sarah Meitner, and to think that he must have known about her infidelity all along. I swallowed hard, and when I looked up from the letter, my eyes were stinging with tears.

"When was this written?"

"Perhaps a month ago, sir."

"So he's dead then, isn't he?"

"I'm afraid so."

"And the boy David?"

"It is said he will be put on the Kinder transport."

"The what?"

"It's a train loaded with children, sir. Germany is sending some of her children out of the country because a world war is imminent. And before she died, Salma signed over all that was left of her assets to secure a place on the train for the child. That was her dying request. The White Angel is dead, sir, but her blood lives on in that boy."

"Where will the train be going then?"

"There's one going through Austria and another through Sweden, but I trust the boy will be on one going into Holland, sir."

* * * * *

"What have I done, Lord, to have disaster follow me like this!" Clarissa wailed when I informed her of the doctor's passing.

"First, my big university-educated son, him gone go marry a Jew, not to say that she not nice. But my God, couldn't him have found a Jamaican? Is what me saying anyway, Agustus is not even Jamaican, but the Good Lord know what I mean. But me shouldn't be too hard on the boy, at least him still come to the house and things like that. But now, Dr. Meitner, who has done so much for us, has passed along. Have mercy, Lord! Is a good thing I have the twin them, and Agustus, 'cause I wouldn't know how to cope."

* * * * *

"John, I hope the connection is good. I can hear static on the line, can you? Mamma told me that the doctor has passed away. I hope you are alright. I'm coming over to be with you and Mary Ambrose. It's strange, John, but I miss him already. Ruth rather liked him, too, not just because he was a Jew, but because she felt that he was decent. Ruth has been a real support. And you know what, John? People here feel that war is going to break out. Did you hear that our prime minister, Neville Chamberlain, went over to Germany and signed the Munich Pact? We all know that our army is no match for Hitler's massive one. Dr. Meitner is almost lucky he didn't live to see this happen. As for me, though, I want to go back home more than ever. The tension is too much for me, John, and I hope for God's sake that we get out before a war. Ruth says she would be happy to go anywhere with me, so I have been extremely lucky."

* * * * *

"Good morning, Mr. Moneague. This is a pleasure, though the circumstances are sad ones. I have been expecting you. Please have a seat. Dr. Meitner has left a box of papers for you to go over. Please read them carefully. I am here to answer any questions you might have, and to clarify any clauses that appear complex."

I looked into the face of Jules Maxwell and saw a handsome and honest man and a potential friend. He motioned to me to sit in a chair at a table over by a window in a room adjoining his office. Looking out the window, I saw a view of the Thames, which brought back memories of my Chelsea room. The trees outside were just as lush and the boats as busy. A flock of birds flew overhead. How things have changed, I thought, for now I know the names of those birds. They are starlings.

"Thank you, Mr. Maxwell," I said huskily, and settled to the task at hand.

Many of the documents were deeds, others were ownership papers and rental receipts. But my first surprise was there in writing. Dr. Meitner, according to these papers, actually owned the flat that Mr. Brown and Clarissa lived in. No wonder their rent was cheap and had never increased in all these years.

There were three envelopes at the bottom of the box. One was tied with a frayed yellow ribbon, one in blue, and the other ribbon seemed new and red. All the envelopes were labelled "John." I opened the one with the yellow ribbon first. A slip of paper fell out, and it read: "This note is from a coward." I extracted the

178

carefully folded note. I stood up slowly, and went over to the window. Pale sunlight fell over the note.

Please forgive me, John. I have been too much of a coward, and I could not bear to lose you. Please remember as you read this that you were the only son I ever had, and I have loved you dearly, though you are not a Jew. But what you have done and continue to do for my people cannot be repaid. I wanted to love and keep you always and, as a result, I have been such a fool. I have kept information from you all these years. Please find it in your heart to still love me. John, I know where to find Miss Shaw. She has been working in the largest research library in New York, in the archives. She is head of the department of Folk and Traditional Tales from Many Lands. I have known this for several years, as had Sarah. It was a bone of contention between us, and after Sarah was gone, I, fool that I was, still held onto the secret.

But now that you are reading this, John, I must have departed from this world, so everything is now out in the open and all is in your hands. I can only hope, my son, that you can still find it in your heart to love me. Your loving father,

Edvard Meitner

I was too stunned for tears, too stunned to cry out. My whole body grew cold and I trembled in the noonday sunlight, and I realized with some surprise that I had been in the office all morning. I didn't know what to think or feel. My breath came out in small gasps and finally, I sat down again and buried my head in my arms, unmindful of Mr. Maxwell in the adjoining room.

The next thing I knew, Mr. Maxwell's secretary was standing over me with a glass of water.

"Here, drink this, or would you rather have a shot of brandy?"

179

"I'm not finished here," I said foolishly, then took the glass from her outstretched hand.

Miss Shaw, Miss Shaw, I thought to myself. I have found you at last!

I sipped the water slowly, and could barely find the strength to read the contents of the envelope tied in blue.

It was Dr. Meitner's last will and testament. He had not forgotten any of us, not even Mary Ambrose. The house was to be given to Mary Ambrose and her brother, Brian. The paintings, including the priceless "The Green Nude," were to be given to Mr. Brown and Clarissa. The antique furnishings were to be given to Gerald and Ruth, and the bulk of his estate was for me to distribute as I saw fit. My first thought was to donate something to the war effort, as well as something to the refugees' cause, because it was no secret that Britain was almost bankrupt. Such a donation would have brought the doctor such pleasure. And remembering the piano at my childhood school, I thought to leave a similarly fitting memorial to the doctor, to be housed at the Jewish Centre for Refugees. I could already see the words I would have inscribed: "This piano is donated to all Jews of the world, whom I have served and loved.

In loving memory of Dr. Edvard Meitner, my father. From his loving son, John Winston Moneague. Such a hero, as he was, should not be forgotten."

* * * * *

The third envelope was a note from Salma, written before her departure. She had left a sum of five thousand pounds in trust for her brother in case he made it to England. She had willingly risked some of the bulk of her estate to ensure his safe passage.

* * * * *

"Miss Clarissa, my dearest! Did you hear what John said? We are the owners of 'The Green Nude.' It is a miracle! And we will even be able to buy a house now. Bethnal Green is no place for a lady like 'The Green Nude,' is it? She deserves much better than this. So do you and the children, Clarissa. We have to thank Dr. Meitner for the rest of our lives, not only for trusting us with its care, but for giving us this opportunity to have a better life."

* * * * *

"Jesus, Mary, Joseph!! John, I can't believe this is me own house. Three bedrooms and all! But what you'se going be doing, John? I wish you would stay. I swear to God I'll be nice. You'se been like a wonderful brother, you know that, don't you? Can't wait to tell me brother Brian. He can come live here with me and all."

"Mary, I'm going to stay here for a little while, but not too long, though. I have something I have to see to. You might have heard that synagogues and Jewish businesses were destroyed over in Germany. Things couldn't be any worse for the Jews there, but I'm still hoping that Salma's young nephew got out before all this evil began to spread. I know Salma would have liked me to try my best to help him, so, Mary, I might be here for less than a year, but after that, I'm going home."

"Home to Jamaica, John? God Almighty, I thought England was your home now."

CHAPTER 23

Refugees

I t wasn't until 1939 before I was able to track down Miss Shaw. She had gone on sabbatical to the Yukon, with no forwarding address, but was expected to return to her position at the library in a few months. That New York Library probably grew disgruntled with my constant pestering.

I was alone when I made the first transatlantic phone call. However, the line was bad. There were static sounds and strange noises, which I naïvely imagined was the ocean. Later that day I implored the operator to try again. She did so with some reluctance, reminding me that an overseas call could cost a fortune.

"I'll pay the fortune!" I shouted into the receiver. "This is urgent!"

Mary Ambrose came into the room stealthily.

"Good God! Don't you be shouting in my house." She poked me in the ribs, laughing. I waved her off, but she went to sit in a chair nearby, no doubt to listen in.

"We have made a connection with the New York Library, sir," the operator said in a clipped accent. I was so nervous that the telephone shook in my hand.

"Hello, may I speak with Miss Fiona Shaw? I'm calling from London, England."

I could hear voices in the background as my heart raced. A woman with an American accent was speaking rapidly.

"Fiona," she said, "it's for you. It's a man, and he sounds marvellously British."

"Hello," said a voice I barely recognized. The static started and my hands sweated.

"Miss Shaw," I said, "it's John."

"John? John who?"

"John Moneague. Remember me?"

* * * * *

Miss Shaw arrived in England a week after my call. She insisted on staying in a hotel in Russell Square, and would not allow me to cover her expenses. She laughingly told me that she was independent and quite capable of managing on her own. However, the New York Library had insisted on covering all her living expenses for a period of three months as long as she would devote some of her time to valuable research.

I was so nervous that I didn't know how to face her alone, and I don't know how many times Elizabeth crossed my mind. In the end, I went alone.

Miss Shaw arranged to meet me in the lush public garden at the square, which I thought fitting since I always associated her with flowers. We were to meet at an ornate gazebo with low benches inside.

It was a shady afternoon, though cool, and flowers were still in bloom. A few birds pecked at seeds left by passersby. Lush trees seemed to lean down to comfort me as I walked nervously across the grass beneath them. I was dressed in an expensive suit and an appropriate tie, and wondered if I should have worn my hat. I was full of memories and anxious. Feeling lightheaded, I placed one foot hesitantly in front of the other, and then I saw her.

There was no mistaking her hair or her pale colouring. It wasn't until I was almost abreast of her that she realized who I was. In my haste to catch up with her, I had forgotten that I had become a man, and she perhaps was expecting a ten-year-old boy.

"Hello," I said, my nervousness disguised, my voice coming out rich and resonant. "It's Miss Shaw isn't it?"

"Are you John?" Her eyes widened with surprise as she moved toward me.

"Yes, it's John Moneague," I said as we locked each other in an embrace.

* * * * *

Miss Shaw remained in England much longer than her planned three months. She came to Mile End Road to see where I lived, and asked me to take her to see Elizabeth.

Elizabeth had no telephone, so there was no way to warn her. When we arrived at her East India Dock Road flat, we caught her completely by surprise. Her hands were covered with clay, and though she had placed old newspapers around her tiny sitting room, splatters from the clay had fallen on all the furnishings. She was embarrassed by the untidiness, but Miss Shaw turned a blind eye, and it was an emotional meeting.

"How beautiful you are, Elizabeth! Look at your hair, how it frames your face. And your son Charlie—what a charmer he is. How wonderful it is to see you again."

"You have not changed a bit yourself, Miss Shaw. You are lovelier than ever. Are you married then?"

Miss Shaw laughed easily. "Not at all. I never found anyone that I would have liked to spend the rest of my life with. I suppose at forty-four you might consider me over the hill, but I feel exactly the same as when you last saw me. So how's your life been, young lady? I hope you are happy."

There was no hiding the sadness in Elizabeth's eyes, and Miss Shaw hurriedly changed the subject.

"Look, I've asked John to come to stay with me at the Russell

184

Hotel while I'm here. It will make it feel more like old times. I know that John has his own finances now, but how wonderful it would be to share the same space again and to wake up and look for him in the mornings like I used to. Remember, John? But you and Charlie are welcome to come, too, anytime. In fact, I would welcome it. It would be so good for all of us to be pampered the way they pamper you there."

"Do you really mean that?" Elizabeth said, wiping her hands in a rag and staring out the window at the rundown London dock. "I suppose a change would be nice."

She avoided my eyes, and I wondered if she knew how I felt about her.

The Russell Hotel was a Victorian grand hotel, complete with cherubs, balconies, and marble columns. How like the old days it felt to stay in the same suite as Miss Shaw. The rooms were flamboyant and spacious, but also provided privacy, if we chose it. It lifted my spirits whenever Miss Shaw and I looked out over the square onto the beautiful garden below.

* * * * *

One afternoon, when it had started to turn cold, we went out on the balcony in thick jackets and talked about our past together, and how Mrs. Arlington had gone senile. Inevitably, our conversations turned to the Meitners and the Jewish cause, and how they had kept from me the fact that Miss Shaw had tried several times to locate me.

"Do you know what, John?" Miss Shaw leaned lightly against me, her hair soft as clouds against my cheek, as her cool hands grasped mine. "I'm so glad that we found each other again. All that business with the Meitners is forgiven. Let's look to the future. But John, there is no hiding the fact that though you are passionate about the Jewish cause, you still have not found contentment. Would it have anything to do with the fact that you are so in love with Elizabeth?"

185

"How did you know?" I asked, holding her hand more tightly, as though afraid that at any moment she might be gone again.

"Women know these things," she said softly, and she might have said even more were it not that a bellboy came to the door to announce that there was a gentleman waiting to see me in the lobby. I was puzzled as to who it could be, but when I took the lift downstairs, I immediately recognized the man in the sea captain's hat who had brought Dr. Meitner's letter.

"Mr. Moneague," he said with a rasp, looking particularly out of place in his shabby seaman's clothing. "Let's go into the garden. We will be less conspicuous."

Out in the garden, he hunched his shoulders against the weather and spoke in such a low tone that I had to lean forward to hear.

"The woman at the house told me where to find you. But listen carefully, sir," he said. "None of this is written down, so you have to remember. The boy we spoke about will be taken into Holland."

"David Heyliger?"

"Yes, he is on a Kinder transport and will be met by a group called 'Youth Aliyah' in Holland. The contact person is Menachem Salter. There will be journalists and photographers meeting the train. As a journalist you can infiltrate the crowds there. The boy will be wearing a red cap. He is blond. His mother was German. You'll recognize him. There are no toilets on the train, no water fountains or anything. He will probably be filthy and miserable. He is almost four years old."

"Where exactly in Holland is the train going, and when does it arrive?"

"It will arrive in about a day or two, sir, at the station in Rotterdam. It would have been sooner if they were not making stops to pick up more passengers. And another thing, Mr. Moneague, I wouldn't be surprised if the boy is released to fair-skinned relatives, if he has any, seeing that he looks German. But

I have a set of false papers for three people—two men and a woman. Use them as you see fit. You might be wanting them, but the rest is up to you, sir."

"Will you be able to take me across to Holland? I presume you are a seaman."

"Yes, sir. I'll do anything for the White Angel, who saved me and my family. Many of us refugees have made a living memorial dedicated to her. We have planted a garden of white roses, and will erect a monument, too."

"A fine honour indeed. What's your name then?"

"Israel Gabin. Some call me 'Captain Isra.' My brother Tobias was the one I told you about. He was married to the angel, but here, take this slip of paper, sir. You can reach me at that number. We can make the rest of the arrangements then. And by the way, if Menachem Salter so much as mentions my name, be sure to make a comment about his watch."

*****

Miss Shaw was very excited when I told her of the purpose of Israel Gabin's visit. She scrutinized herself in front of a full-length mirror.

"I think I could pass as an aunt or something. I could pull my hair back the way those European women do, and wear one of those ugly scarves that make them all look like peasants. But first I have to go to the Clothes Barrel. It's a cheap store I saw over in the East End that sells second-hand garments. I'll be needing shoes—sturdy ones—a plain old dress, and a coat like those worn by farmers' wives. None of this American razzmatazz will do over there. I'll ask Elizabeth to come shopping with me."

I had never seen Miss Shaw look so lovely, her cheeks smooth and pink with excitement, and her eyes shining as she tugged at her lovely hair. I knew it would be useless to try to dissuade her, for when I thought about it, it was thanks to her that I was so comfortable in assuming identities. This mission, of course, could prove dangerous because we were not play-acting, as we did in the old days. This was real.

"First, I have to see my lawyer," I said quickly. "I want to make sure that things are in order in case anything happens. I have a large amount of money to consider, as well as properties."

"May I accompany you, John? I hope you don't mind, but there is something in me that still wants to look out for you."

"I don't mind at all. In fact, I would welcome it."

"Let's see those identity cards. What are our names to be, John?"

"Helga Linsstrom, and Burnt Jurgens. We are brother and sister. You are married to Freidrick Linsstrom, a Swedish fisherman. I am single and work in a cheese factory over in Jutland, Denmark. The child is going to England with us, where we are going to settle. We have papers to prove that also. We do not have to speak German or Dutch because they will ask language of preference. We will say English, and we'll speak in heavily accented English."

"Well, let's start practising then, John. We have no time to lose."

* * * * *

It was Saturday, but Mr. Maxwell was kind enough to open his office for us. I was unprepared for the attention that he paid Miss Shaw. He brought tea and biscuits into the meeting room. And as I sat, going over my papers, he came into the room, looking young and rakish. A lock of his dark hair fell sensually over his green eyes, and it somehow accented his distinctive profile and reminded me of a handsome gypsy.

"Call me Jules," he said to Miss Shaw. "How long will you be staying in London?"

"It depends," she replied coyly. "I have a few errands, of course, but other than that, who knows?"

"Forgive me, Miss Shaw, if I'm stepping out of line, but would you like to join me for a drink this evening? Or would that be an intrusion on Mr. Moneague?"

"Not at all. John and I are old friends. It's been about fifteen years now, John, hasn't it? I'd love to join you. I'm sure John wouldn't mind taking the opportunity to see some of his friends while I'm gone."

"Splendid," he said. "It's settled then. I'll pick you up at your hotel at six-thirty."

Seeing the look of adoration in Jules Maxwell's eyes made me wonder for a moment if he was aware that Miss Shaw was at least fourteen years his senior. But then again, seeing the spark that ignited between them, I didn't suppose age would have mattered.

"I was a child when I first met Miss Shaw," I said.

"You must have both been children. Did you meet in Jamaica then?"

"Yes, Jules, we met in Jamaica, but John was a student of mine. Please feel free to call me Fiona."

* * * * *

That evening, I called Gerald from the hotel, wondering if he would like to go out to a pub, but he was studying and, to make matters worse, Ruth's parents were coming over to his flat in Hampstead for the first time. Then I thought of Elizabeth. She was the reason I had even bothered to see Jules Maxwell. I wanted to be sure that if anything happened to me, she would be provided for.

"I'm wearing this little black number." Miss Shaw came into the room, wearing a spaghetti-strap black dress that fell to her ankles. How attractive she looked with her hair falling in ringlets about her shoulders and her slim figure outlined. On her ears was a pair of diamond earrings.

"These are fake," she said, pointing to the earrings, "but everything else is real. Do I look alright?"

"You couldn't look better." I said, and meant it.

"Why don't you go visit with Elizabeth?" she suggested. "You both could use the company, and her husband is away all the time. If you ask me, I don't even think they are actually a couple. Being cooped up in that flat with a kid all day must be so boring for her. Tell her to live a little and bring them over here, order room service, if you want to. And, John, I have a feeling I won't be home tonight. In fact I might as well tell you right now. I won't."

✳ ✳ ✳ ✳ ✳

I found Elizabeth reading a story to Charlie. I saw them through the window before I knocked hesitantly at her door. She smiled when she saw me and asked me to come in. Almost all at once, Charlie was in my arms and the book was quite forgotten.

"Would you like a cup of tea?" Elizabeth asked.

"That would be great. I actually came to invite you and Charlie over to the hotel where Miss Shaw and I are staying."

"Are you serious? Have you seen our clothes? That place is so posh, John!"

"Elizabeth," I said, brashly, "your clothes are clean and so are Charlie's, but if it makes you feel better, there's time to change if you want to. I'm in no hurry."

"If you think we are alright as we are, I'll just pull on a light coat and Charlie can put on his jacket."

I couldn't believe that finally I would have a chance to spend a few hours in Elizabeth's company. Not wanting to waste a moment, I hailed a cab on the High Street, which took us directly to the hotel.

The doorman nodded at me. "Mr. Moneague," he mumbled in a friendly manner. "Is he a soldier?" Charlie asked loudly. "My daddy's a soldier."

We crossed the lobby and took the lift up to the suite, where Charlie entertained us with airplane noises. Elizabeth could not believe how large the suite was.

"This is larger than my whole flat!" she exclaimed, her eyes wide as I gave them a tour of our spacious bedrooms, sitting room, dining room, bar, reading room, and wide balcony. "What an amazing place. Just look at the fabulous furnishings and rugs. It must cost a fortune!"

I laughed and took Charlie over to the radio and switched it on. There were some spluttering sounds, then a voice came on and Charlie looked behind the radio, wondering where the man was.

Elizabeth and I looked at each other and smiled. Neither of us knew what to say. When I turned the radio off, Charlie said that the man had gone to sleep. Then he said that he was hungry, so I ordered room service.

"What are we going to do if war comes?" Elizabeth asked unexpectedly. I poured her a glass of the best French white wine and put a finger to my lips.

"Let's not spoil the evening for Charlie. I'm going to look after you both, so don't you worry."

Charlie ate his supper of sausage rolls and salmon and a few helpings of cheese, followed by a slice of rich chocolate cake and lemonade.

"I'm stuffed, Mummy," he said, going over to look out the window overlooking the garden.

"Want to go for a walk down there?" I suggested, standing beside him.

"No thanks, I'm sleepy." He stifled a yawn.

"Well, I guess we'd better go then." Elizabeth got up from the sofa and smoothed her skirt.

"Don't go, please," I said quickly. "There's a small couch in the reading room. It's a daybed, and Charlie can sleep there. I'll fetch some blankets and a pillow."

"I don't want to put you to any trouble, John, on my account. Are you sure it's alright?"

"Of course I'm sure, Elizabeth. Miss Shaw wouldn't mind at all."

* * * * *

The moment Charlie fell off to sleep, Elizabeth became agitated.

"Oh my God, John, haven't you heard people saying that England is going to be at war soon? I know that London is sure to be a target for bombs, and with us living so close to the docks.... Oh, John, don't you think the Germans might be bent on cutting off Britain's supplies by destroying our shipyards?"

"Elizabeth, if what you are saying is true, we might never have another night like this, and I have so many things to say to you. Please, not another word about the war. Let me speak from my heart. I love you very much, and have felt that way ever since I saw you at my puppet show that day. My God, Elizabeth, you don't know how I have agonized. I didn't want to interfere with your marriage, but I can't stop myself from loving you."

I poured myself a glass of wine and another for Elizabeth. She sipped at hers slowly, not saying a word. Then I poured her another, and she moved closer to me on the couch. I put my arms around her.

"I promise that I'll keep you and Charlie safe."

I felt her snuggle even closer, and I couldn't stop myself. I kissed her lips, and stroked her long beautiful hair. She offered no resistance.

"John, I've loved you since we were children. That's why I never forgot your name," she said simply.

192

I lifted her and took her to my room, and she felt as light as the down in my soft covers.

* * * * *

The next morning, Charlie came to find us. "Mummy," he said, climbing up to join us in bed, "I'm hungry."

It was almost eleven. We reluctantly got up, washed, and went downstairs to the breakfast room. There were kippers, sausages, black pudding, pickled herring, and eggs to choose from, as well as scones, toast, marmalade, cream, and jam.

"I wish they had fried dumplings," I said jokingly, which amused Elizabeth. It was nice to hear her laugh and see her eyes light up.

"You're a real Jamaican, though you look so English."

We were having toast and marmalade and scones with cream when one of the waiters came into the room and announced that some important news was about to be broadcast. We all fell silent, even Charlie. The waiter plugged in the radio and turned up the volume. The voice that came on was anguished, and it was a moment before we realized that it was the voice of our prime minister, Mr. Chamberlain.

"I have to tell you," he said, "that … that this country is at war with Germany."

* * * * *

Miss Shaw returned home just after midday, accompanied by Jules Maxwell. They, too, had heard the news and were as upset as we were.

"Germany might start bombing the city," Jules Maxwell said. "No one is safe. It is not going to matter what class you are. As far as they are concerned, we are all English. You might be safer going back to America, Fiona, my dear. I couldn't bear to think what could happen."

"No, darling. Thanks for your concern. You are a wonderful man, Jules, but I've never played safe. There are things I promised John that I would do and, God help me, I'll do them."

"Fiona, I'm worried for you, that's all. But please, if you need any help with whatever it is you are planning to do, I hope you know you can trust me. I can help. You only need ask."

"Do you speak Dutch or German then?"

"I know a smattering of both. Why?"

"We might need you then, darling. John, what do you think? Shouldn't we tell Elizabeth and Jules why we are going to Holland tomorrow night?"

"I guess we have no choice. Elizabeth is aware of how much I love her, and I can't help but noticing that you seem to have developed feelings for Mr. Maxwell."

* * * * *

By one o'clock that afternoon, Elizabeth and I and Charlie took a taxi back to her flat, and I noticed she was shivering.

"Are you alright? Here—use my coat. It will warm you up."

"John, that won't help. You know I won't be happy until you return safely, don't you?"

"Is daddy going to war too, Mummy?" Charlie said, "He's a soldier, you know."

"Yes, your daddy's going to war, too," I said, "but everything is going to be alright, isn't it Elizabeth?"

"For God sakes, John, you be careful. I'm so nervous thinking of all the things that could go wrong on your mission."

"What mission, Mummy? Is Uncle John going to war, too?"

"Hush, Charlie. Uncle John's right. Everything's going to be okay. Now go to your room and play. Uncle John and I need to talk."

"Can I show Uncle John my toys after?"

"Sure, now off with you."

"Elizabeth, nothing will go wrong. Miss Shaw and I have had lots of experience working together and besides, Jules will be there with guns if needed."

"I wish I could be with you, John."

"Next you'll be wanting to bring Charlie too." I grinned. "You both must stay at Miss Shaw's hotel while we are away. It's somewhat safer there. All of London is preparing for air raids. There are shelters all over the city, and gas masks are being issued. Did you hear those sirens on the radio earlier? That's what the air raid warning will sound like. If you hear it, quickly put on your and Charlie's gas masks and head for the shelter. And don't turn the radio off. Listen for bulletins. I have called Mary Ambrose. She and her brother, Brian, are going to stay at the hotel with you. They're nervous about being over here in the East End as well. Clarissa and Mr. Brown want to stay with Gerald and Ruth. Clarissa says they will be praying for everyone's safety. Don't forget what I said. Keep safe. I love you and will come back to you."

* * * * *

The next evening, Israel Gabin was supposed to be waiting for us near the canal, which ran beside the West India Dock. He was nowhere to be seen, and the shipyards were deserted. The only occasional sounds were of a distant radio and the noxious swearing of a drunken sailor.

"Good evening, Mr. Moneague," Captain Isra said, stepping out from the gloom, surprising us. "We have to wait until it's darker because with the war and all, the boats coming and going are being watched more carefully. I have brought black raincoats for everyone. They will help to blend us into the night, but there's a crawl space at the bottom of my boat. It is well disguised for occasions such as this. It's a close fit, but it will hold you all and the boy, too, when we get him. I have learned that someone called Norbert Wollheim is the one who arranged his transport. But if

195

you need help, contact the Joodsche Raad—it is the Jewish council in Rotterdam. It is said that every child on the train was given a small suitcase and a number. David's will be number 202. But at all costs, try not to arouse suspicions. Don't worry about me— I have made this trip a dozen times. No harm in us having a drop of tea now, though, for we won't be eating again until we get to Holland."

We followed the captain nervously into a ramshackle warehouse, where he retrieved a thermos from an abandoned crate and a couple of chipped enamel mugs.

"I'll share with Jules," said Miss Shaw, eyeing the unwashed mugs.

From the inside of his jacket, Captain Isra drew out a long thin loaf of bread, which he broke into four pieces.

"You'll be needing this, too. It's cold and choppy out there. This will help to warm you up."

It drizzled for most of the evening, and every now and again the sounds of a lone airplane alarmed us. Each time we heard it, we thought it might be a bomber. The moon was behind clouds when we pushed off, and from beneath the crawl space, I felt the damp seeping in. The three of us—Jules, Miss Shaw, and I—were all shivering from the cold as we held on to each other, and the boat valiantly broke over the surf. I don't know how long we were aboard, but it seemed like hours. We lay cramped and freezing, and still the boat plunged on. Suddenly there was a loud boom like an explosion.

"What's that?" I whispered, glad to see that we were all still in one piece.

"I don't know," Jules answered.

"Sounded like a mine, didn't it?" Miss Shaw said, holding our hands more tightly. "We have to prepare for the worst."

We heard Israel Gabin's boots pound above us, then he poked his head into the crawl space.

"Sorry," he said, "that was a mine. A boat ahead of us went up with it! This is dangerous territory. It looks as if the explosion caused another boat immediately behind it to turn over. One of its crew members was thrown to safety. He's swimming toward us now. So not a sound, mind you!"

None of us made a sound. We clung together, hoping the sounds of our breathing would not be audible. We felt the boat lurch and heard voices. I thought at first they were speaking English, but quickly realized it was German. Our passenger is German, I thought to myself, and we are all going to die.

I don't know how long it was after that when I felt the boat slow down. Overcome by exhaustion, I dozed off, but awoke to find Miss Shaw still holding on to Jules and me. I felt the boat come to a halt and knew it had moored, but still, none of us dared move. After what must have been the longest twenty minutes of my life, we started off again. We must have been well out to sea when we heard heavy footsteps above us. None of us knew what to expect, and we were terrified. Thankfully, it was Israel Gabin.

"That was a German patrol boat," he said calmly. "Those idiots hit one of their own mines! One of the three crew members in the boat behind them survived. He is the one who came aboard. He says his name is Markus Winkler. He was unharmed by the blast. To avoid suspicion, I dropped him off on Dutch soil, and for all he knows, I am only a fisherman going back out to sea. He was quite talkative and said that Germany plans to invade Poland. He must have thought that I was German, so I humoured him and said that my name was Heinz Werner, and I pretended to be pleased about the recent German invasions. Then he said something that might interest you. He said that Holland wants to be declared a neutral territory in this war. So it is possible that there won't be guns trained on us, but anyway, I would still be cautious. Those bloody Germans have murdered so many civilians. What difference would killing three or four more make?"

When Israel Gabin brought the boat into the harbour in Rotterdam, we finally emerged from our hiding place to find that things around us looked relatively normal. There were no patrols or hidden artillery. It was clear that the war with Germany had not yet touched Holland's soil. I felt disadvantaged in not speaking the language. Israel Gabin was able to exchange greetings with a few Dutch seamen, who were already along the wharf in spite of the hour. When we came to the end of the dock, Israel Gabin wished us Godspeed and said he would be back to pick us up early the next morning.

Finally, realizing that we were on our own, I couldn't help but speculate on all that could happen to us before then. Every sound, every whisper, our simplest movements, the cool dry wind, and even the sea's ferocity seemed potentially dangerous. Even more disconcerting was the fact that Rotterdam seemed unaffected by the war in neighbouring Europe. Its bakeries were open, as were the cheese shops and even clothing stores.

Sturdy bridges spanned the canals that were all over the city, and almost every bridge was broad enough to support pedestrians, cyclists, automobiles, and possibly even an invading army.

We all felt more than a touch of bravado as we wandered the as yet empty streets. Only a few women were already up at this early hour, cleaning steps and sidewalks, oblivious of the impending danger of war. Some even shouted at us as we sauntered past, and Jules insisted that they were wishing us a good day, but from the way they shook their washcloths at us, I wasn't sure of that.

We made our way quietly through old and narrow cobbled streets without attracting undue attention, and finally approached the train station, following Israel Gabin's detailed instructions. The streets grew unexpectedly crowded with cyclists, and it became obvious that we were among the few who did not have bicycles. Jules slowed his pace and pointed to a sign, which read "Erwtensoep" and glanced at his watch.

"Hungry?" he asked. "That sign means pea soup, so let's have something to eat. It's an hour before the train anyway."

"Have you got any Dutch currency?" I asked, suddenly remembering that English bank notes might well prove useless in Rotterdam.

"Yes, I have guilders. Let's go inside, shall we?"

Miss Shaw and I sat together, not saying anything, at a table in a corner, leaving Jules to deal with the ordering. When he returned, he said that the woman at the counter was wondering where we were from.

"What did you say?" I whispered, and I felt more than one pair of eyes scrutinizing us. Miss Shaw certainly looked like a countrywoman with her scarf, frumpy coat, and thick-soled shoes, while Jules and I, in our cheap suits, could easily have been a pair of country bumpkins.

"I said we were from far away, near Groningen, but you two had been living in Sweden and Denmark and have forgotten most of your Dutch."

Miss Shaw stifled a laugh, but could not hide the admiration in her eyes.

"Jules, darling," she whispered, "you are so darn good at this game, it's scary. How on earth did you come up with that name anyway?"

"It was easy. I once spent a summer there as a child. From what I remember of it, it was in the middle of nowhere."

"Brilliant, darling."

No sooner than she said that when two German officers entered the café and began to read out loud from the menu, translating it into German.

"Kaffee, Nachtisch, Geback, Obstkuchen, Salat, Forelle, Suppe."

"Hush," I said, "we mustn't let them hear us speaking in English."

The two officers looked over in our direction and nodded. I was certain they recognized us as frauds, but then they smiled and ordered the same soup we were having.

"We've got to get out of here," Jules hissed. "The train must have come in. That's why those officers are here."

"Guten Tag," the officers said in German as we went by.

"Guten Tag," we replied, imitating their accents. But one of them put his arm out and barred Miss Shaw's way.

"You very pretty," he said in broken English. "Verstehen Sie mich?"

"I thank you," replied Miss Shaw in heavily accented English, not understanding a word of his German.

He smiled and let us pass. As soon as we were outside, we began to hurry. Swarms of reporters and photographers were waiting at the train station, all eager for news of the latest developments in Germany. Jules assumed the role of a journalist, using his fake identification card, and quickly joined their ranks, while Miss Shaw and I stood with a crowd that we assumed were prospective parents and relatives. An officer came out on to the platform and motioned to all of us to follow. We ended up in a room that reminded me of those I had been cross-examined in in England.

Everyone was expected to file past a large desk, where all our identification cards were looked over by two officers.

"Language of choice?" they asked, speaking in English, barely moving their lips.

"The English," Miss Shaw replied, holding tightly to my hand. A pair of ice blue eyes looked into Miss Shaw's face, and the officer said, "Many of these kinder are en route to Israel. You must speak to Menachem Salter of Youth Aliyah at the desk on the right."

We were ushered into a room with no chairs, just a large desk. The man before us looked tired and beaten.

"I'm Menachem Salter," he said, standing to acknowledge us.

"We are here for helping David Heyliger, number 202," I said, keeping my voice as level as possible.

"Will you be accompanying him to Israel? Are you relatives?"

"No, I plan not to go to Israel. I'm boy's uncle."

"Why is your name not Heyliger? Are you his mother's brother?"

"No, I am father's half brother. My mother's disgrace sent us to Holland and Denmark."

"Who's this woman?"

"My sister. She will help raise child."

Menachem Salter hunched over our identification cards briefly, shook his head, and looked up at us with disbelief.

"Your sister, eh? Are you married then, lady?"

"Yes, husband was farmer in Sweden," Miss Shaw replied. "He die, so I go live with this my brother Burnt."

"Where do you plan to raise the boy, if not Israel?"

"The England," I replied. "Here, my affidavit. I get job in tannery. We take boat to the England."

"Good," Menachem Salter said pensively. "Is there any chance your captain might be called Israel?"

"Nice watch you wear. Swiss?" I asked, remembering the instructions from Captain Isra. Neither Miss Shaw nor I responded to or even flinched at his question about the captain, though I sensed something was quite different about Menachem Salter's attitude toward us.

"Yes, it's a very good watch," he said softly, "almost as good as the captain's."

He didn't say anything after that and subtly motioned to us to leave the room. We were told to proceed to platform 5. Though we dared not look back, we knew his eyes were on us still, and Miss Shaw and I walked out to the platform together, backs straight, holding each other's hands in a firm grip. There was no way to tell, I thought, who might or might not be a traitor.

* * * * *

The train doors opened. The children filed out and stood around in groups. All their eyes looked frightened, though older children were trying to comfort the younger ones. There were numbers written on cards hung around their necks, and their only

201

luggage was a small black suitcase that could barely hold a change of clothing.

We searched among them frantically. There must have been over two hundred children, but it was Miss Shaw who found him. He looked filthy as expected, and he was sitting on his suitcase, sucking his thumb and crying.

"David," she said, "don't cry. I'm here now."

* * * * *

Miss Shaw lifted him up, and he buried his fair head in her hair and wrapped his skinny arms around her neck. His nose needed wiping, and his cheeks were stained with tears. We walked quickly along the platform and were again stopped by an official who proceeded to stamp all our documents. It seemed a hundred years before we were once more outside the building.

"Let's find Jules," Miss Shaw said. "The child is hungry, and also we must find a place to stay the night."

Suddenly I heard someone running behind us. I struggled to appear calm.

"Perhaps it's Jules," I said.

We slowed our pace, and a fair-haired young man, no older than I, drew abreast of us.

"Good day," he said in English. "I'm Neils Welen. I wear a fine watch, see?" He held his arm out and showed us a beat-up silver watch.

"One day I'm going to put a diamond near the watch face because it will brighten it up. It's old, yes? It used to belong to my grandfather. I give you his address. You will be safe if you stay for the night in the home of Josef Van Dijk. Here, take the address. He has hot meal waiting for boy."

Before we could thank him for the slip of paper he handed to us, he ran off and soon blended in with the crowds.

"I wonder if we can trust him," I said out loud, and then

202

remembered that he had made a point of mentioning his watch and felt more reassured.

Jules was sitting on a bench among a group of foreign photographers, looking genuinely interested in their equipment. When he saw us approach, he stood up quickly.

"Fiona, darling, thank God you are safe. Is the boy alright? Let's have a look at him. What a beautiful boy!"

"I'm his mother now," Miss Shaw said matter of factly, still holding the child. "He doesn't have anyone else."

That night, we arrived at the home of Josef Van Dijk. He was exactly as I had imagined him—grey-haired, round glasses, red-faced, and portly. He shook our hands as though we were old friends.

"Come in," he said. "You are most welcome here."

Josef Van Dijk's home had looked narrow from the outside, but once indoors, we found the rooms spacious. The wood-panelled walls and comfortable furniture lent an air of relaxed domesticity. I was surprised when we were shown a sliding door, which had resembled a wall. Behind it was a steep wooden staircase leading to the attic through a concealed trap door.

"Things will get worse here in Holland before it gets any better," he explained, noticing my unease. "That's why I take precautions now to prepare for the future. There are two mattresses up there, a sink for washing, and a toilet. Also, I made a pot of borscht, and there is bread and cheese and a jug of the freshest Dutch milk. Please accept my humble hospitality. In the morning, there is no need to wake me when you leave. May God go with you, my friends."

We thanked him, and though we offered payment, he would not accept.

"You would have done the same for me."

How far away England and Elizabeth felt that night.

*****

We awoke early the next morning. The boy David and I had shared a mattress, though we pulled the two mattresses together so that he would also feel close to Miss Shaw. He rubbed his eyes and pointed at the bread and cheese.

"Brot, kase," he said.

We broke the bread and shared the cheese among us and ate in silence, then washed it all down with milk before heading out into the cool morning air.

"All we have to do now is find Captain Israel," said Jules. "It is dark, though, so I hope we will be able to find his boat."

"He seems a man of his word," I said. "He will wait for us no matter what."

Jules hoisted young David up on his shoulders and walked with long strides. In less than no time, we were down at the shipyard. The streets were deserted. "Can you see anything of the captain?" asked Miss Shaw anxiously, perhaps having noticed that all the boats lined up looked almost identical.

"No, darling, he's evidently not here," replied Jules as he and I hastily peered into each boat, hoping to recognize something familiar. After a while, our efforts seemed useless.

We heard heavy footsteps pounding along the wooden wharf where we lingered in the shadows, but it was impossible to make out anything in the dark. "The boat's here, sir," Captain Isra hissed, appearing unexpectedly. "You mustn't go into the crawl space yet. You are being followed. Just sit tight, as though you are going on a nice Sunday picnic."

We all sat leisurely in the boat. Miss Shaw played lazily with a stick in the water, amusing David, as though there was no hurry. Jules surprised me by quietly singing a slow, sad song, and I lay back trying to look carefree, while Captain Isra inspected his fishing gear.

"Guten Morgen," a German voice said. A tall German officer, dressed in full uniform, emerged from the fog. He looked threatening, his hands were on his hips, and his revolver was close at hand. "Es tut mir leid," he said softly.

The captain replied in German. Although I did not understand a word, the conversation sounded amiable. After a few moments, Captain Isra reverted to speaking in English and turned to us.

"This is the man I rescued yesterday, Markus Winkler. How well he looks. I told him we were just leaving on a family fishing trip. Captain Winkler, this is my wife Gretchen, my son Peder, and his uncles Ivan and Derek."

"Nice to meet you. I understand you speak some English, not much German," said the officer, tipping his cap. "You will laugh when I tell you this, but from the distance, I thought you were Jewish refugees, but up close I can see you are all Aryan. I must confess I was very wrong. There is not one Jew among you. I am sorry for the disturbance. Your wife is so lovely, no? Enjoy your outing. Auf Wiedersehen."

CHAPTER 24

I Won't Be Back for Many a Day

When Captain Isra finally pushed off, we all had the distinct feeling that the German officer was still watching us. We continued our charade of a family out on a fishing trip until we were well out to sea.

The sky cleared dramatically and there were bands of orange from the rising sun.

"Don't worry about the mines," said Captain Isra as we finally went below into the crawl space. "I'm familiar with navigating the English Channel. You'll be as safe as a baby in arms. The last thing I'd want is to harm this child."

He broke off speaking and looked skyward. "I hear something! Lie low!" he hissed.

There was no mistaking the roaring sound of fighter planes that grew closer.

"Those are German bombers!" Captain Isra shouted over the roar. "They are heading toward England! Luckily we are not their target—we wouldn't stand a chance. A lone fishing boat would be of no interest, I'd say."

"But what if they intend to bomb London?" I shouted back, grateful that David did not speak English and did not seem to understand the seriousness of what was happening.

"Let's hope for God's sake that the RAF puts a stop to it," said Jules, "or else all of London will be facing terrible danger."

"Try not to alarm the child." Miss Shaw had her arms wrapped lovingly around David. "He might not understand our words, but he's frightened enough as it is already."

We continued to hear the drone of the bombers for such a long time, and I couldn't help but think how vulnerable we were out there on the rough sea. I felt Miss Shaw's hand grip mine reassuringly.

"John, what a fine pair we have been, and look where it's got us." Though my head was turned away, I could almost see her feisty smile, and I gripped her hand tightly in return.

"Fiona," Jules said hesitantly, "if we get through this, consider us lucky. But I can't think of another woman I would have liked spending my last moments with. You are the bravest woman I have ever known."

"Jules, darling, it's strange, but I never thought I'd ever be saying these words to any man, and so soon after meeting him. But now it seems almost too late, if you know what I mean. You have become very dear to me, Jules. It's almost as though I saved the best for last."

The boat heaved and pulled through the water. We couldn't help but wonder what had become of the bombers. None of us said a word, for each of us was immersed in our own troubled thoughts.

"Seems no one is terribly concerned about our small fishing boat," Captain Isra said, sounding somewhat amused when we at last landed on English soil. "We obviously don't look like a threat to anyone. More likely, the army and navy's attention has been diverted by those bombers. Let's get this chap home safely. The spirit of the White Angel is watching over us."

I said a silent prayer in thanksgiving.

* * * * *

The Jewish resistance in London was able to supply David with a set of false papers that provided him with a new identity. He was to be called David Liger Shaw, for Miss Shaw would not part with him and said that the middle name of Liger was to remind him that he once was a Heyliger.

"When I leave England, I'll take David with me. It is strange to think that when I came to England, I had no idea that I was coming here to become a mother."

"Are you going back to America with him?" I asked nervously, remembering our long years of separation and how often I had longed for this reunion.

"No, honey, I won't go back to America this time because I happen to know that you want to go back to Jamaica, and I don't look forward to our being separated again. Since I still have the house and property there, I was thinking that if we can get out of England, that's where I'd go."

"What about Jules then? Is he going with you?"

"Honey, Jules is so much younger than I am. I wouldn't want to pressure him in any way. He still has choices and decisions to make in life that will affect his future. I would feel as though I were denying him his right to do so if I pressed him in any way. So it's entirely up to him, wouldn't you say?"

"Do you love him, Miss Shaw?"

"Strange as it might seem, after only just meeting him, I think I do. We have been through such a traumatic experience together. But all the while, I feared for him and couldn't stand the thought of losing him. I can only hope that he feels the same about me."

* * * * *

"Hello, John, is that you? It's Gerald. Thank God you are home safe. Mamma and I and Ruth were all praying for your safe return. I hope the lot of you are alright, and the boy, too, of course. But, John, have you seen the changes here in London? The children are being evacuated, and there are bomb shelters and gas masks everywhere. It is rather frightening. Ruth and I have been helping out in an infirmary. There are a lot of injured that need seeing to. Thank God so far bombers have passed over the city. There have been no bombs."

"Hello, Gerald. I have only been back a few days now, but you are right—London is almost a ghost town. The sounds of air raid sirens take some getting used to. Thanks for your prayers. We are all safe and the boy, too. You'd think Miss Shaw was his mother the way she fusses over him, but in a good way, mind you. Isn't it heartbreaking, Gerald, to see London's children separated from their parents? I can certainly empathize with their fear as they are packed off on trains to find shelter with strangers out in the country. The world has turned upside down. No wonder I'm planning to go back to Jamaica in November. And I was hoping that you and Ruth would come too. Do you still want to go back?"

"John, I've always said that that was my dream, didn't I? Let's see anyone try and stop me now. In fact, I just heard that there are some wealthy Jews and Syrians in Jamaica establishing businesses in the retail industry. It occurred to me that I would be the ideal person to look after their accounts and investments, and Ruth could help out with the legal side of things. I only just spoke to a Jamaican chap a few days ago named C.B. Grubb, who told me that they are going to be operating stores on centrally located King Street. Remember King Street, John? I can hardly wait to see it again. I will get everything in order."

"What about Clarissa and Mr. Brown?"

"Mamma wouldn't come, John. England is her home now, and the twins are English. This is their country. But as for yourself, what do you plan to do there?"

"Well, Gerald, it would seem that journalists are in high demand these days because these are frightening as well as exciting times that should be chronicled, and the whole world is waiting for information."

209

My mind was in turmoil about contacting Elizabeth. It was not that my feelings for her had changed, but something in me wanted to be decent and not be a slave to my passion. Perhaps that is why I did not return to the hotel where she and Mary Ambrose had been waiting for us. Instead, I took Jules up on an offer to stay with him in Knightsbridge for a few weeks in his Brompton Square home until my departure in November. Inevitably our conversations often turned to Miss Shaw.

"John," he said one morning as we sat in his airy breakfast room, "I'm not old—far from it. In fact, I'm only a few years older than you are, but there are things I crave—not material things, mind you, but more precious things such as companionship and deep affection. Until that day you walked into my office with Fiona, I had thought that all I would get out of life was my work, which I am good at and enjoy, but there's more to life than work. Thank God I have my health, but what I'm really saying is that more than anything, I want to spend every waking hour with that woman. She probably thinks I'm far too young for her, and she might be right, but that doesn't stop me feeling the way I do. Damn this war and the constant fear that we have to live with! And damn America, because America will take her away from me!"

I couldn't help but admire Jules Maxwell for speaking from the heart. "Jules, America will not take her away from you. Speaking as one man to another, I know she has very strong feelings for you, and she is not looking forward to being parted from you. In fact, she wants to return to Jamaica because I want to go back. She and I both feel that now that we have found each other again as friends, we don't want to lose sight of each other again. From what I understand, she loves you. I think her greatest fear is not the war, as you might think, but her fear of losing you."

"You mean she actually loves me? If that's true—and I hope it is—I don't see any reason why I shouldn't ask her if she would mind my travelling with you both to the island."

"I think she would welcome it, Jules."

Two weeks after that conversation, Miss Shaw contacted me early one morning to let me know that Mary Ambrose and her brother had returned to Mile End Road. They had despaired over the war-imposed conditions and concluded that they might as well remain in their own home.

"And what of Elizabeth?" I finally asked, unable to restrain my curiosity.

"Elizabeth's gone back to Limehouse. She took Charlie. She says it might be best that he be evacuated with the other kids in London. She says she didn't want him to be in danger here. But, John, if the truth be told, I think the reason Elizabeth is staying behind here is because of you."

That afternoon, I took a taxi to Limehouse. There was such a sense of gloom and depression everywhere. Children who were left behind in the city looked hollow-eyed and frightened. Old age pensioners seemed the most vulnerable. Many of them had to depend solely on the kindness of neighbours. I climbed the rickety stairs to Elizabeth's flat, but found it deserted and empty.

I went back down the stairs, feeling despondent and unsure of what to do. Then I saw an old Chinese man at the bottom of the stairs beckoning to me. He clearly wanted me to follow him. We went through a maze of back streets and lanes, and finally ended up in front of a ramshackle building, not far from the shipyards. Inside, in the gloom, I made out a set of low cots, where about a dozen or so old Chinese men lay. Then I saw Elizabeth. She was bending over a figure on one of the cots. I hastened to her side and saw that Charlie was asleep at the foot of the bed. Elizabeth was so distraught that she barely acknowledged my presence.

"It's Brandon," she finally said, and I saw that her eyes were swollen and tearful. "He's dead."

"What happened?" I asked, shocked by the emaciated appearance of Elizabeth's husband.

"Brandon deserted the army," Elizabeth said in a whisper. "He was a coward, John. He was keeping another woman in Manchester, and then pretended that she was pregnant. He thought that this would be enough of an excuse to allow him to stay out of the army during the war. His lie was discovered—not that it would have helped him anyway—and he deserted. I didn't know that he had returned here to Limehouse to hide out in this opium den. Apparently, he had been here for over a month, though he never tried to contact us until now. He wanted to say he was sorry for abandoning us, and for drinking and smoking away the last of our money. He said his liver had given out, and he knew that he was dying. I don't know what will become of us now, John, and I don't know what to tell Charlie about him. I am so grateful that you've come. I asked that old man, Yuping Lowe, who brought you here, to keep an eye on my old flat in case you turned up. He promised to bring you directly to me if you did. Everything I had has been stolen. My pottery, my clothes, my furniture, and even Charlie's toys."

"Didn't the army officials come looking for you during that time?"

"No. Brandon no longer considered us married and kept my address secret."

"What will happen to his body then?"

"I have contacted the army officials, and they will take care of all the arrangements."

* * * * *

CHAPTER 25

The Final Solution

"God Almighty, John! Don't you go paying any more money than is necessary. Tell Elizabeth she can stay with me and our Brian on Mile End Road for as long as she will be wanting."

"Thanks, Mary Ambrose. For God's sake, you be careful. Promise that the minute you hear sirens, you'll make it to the nearest shelter. I'm staying with Jules Maxwell, the lawyer, as you might already know, but I'm planning on going back to Jamaica."

"Holy Mother of God! You'se bin the best of friends to me. Is the least I could do isn't it? T'will be such a great treat to be with young Charlie again. When will she be coming then?"

"How about tonight?"

"T'will be a right treat to be sure. But when will you be leaving then for Jamaica?"

"November 12th, and because of the war, we might be forced to travel with refugees. Jews are pouring out from all over Europe, and so many countries are refusing to take them in—England, Cuba, and the United States included."

"God Almighty! What's them refugees to do then? As if being poor is not bad enough, but being poor with no country is a right shame, isn't it?"

"You're right, Mary Ambrose. Luckily some Latin American countries are more generous. Trinidad and the Dominican Republic might take some in also, but it is only because of Captain Isra's connections that this captain has agreed to make a stop in Jamaica's Kingston Harbour as well."

"John, luv, do you think Jamaica would be any better for an uneducated girl like me?"

Mary Ambrose looked very serious. I realized then that leaving England meant leaving friends behind, and a part of my life that never could be recaptured. I reached out and took her in my arms as she sobbed.

"Jesus, Mary, Joseph!" she exclaimed through her tears. "I want to come with you'se all. What would I do without you and Gerald to worry over? Just you tell me!"

"What about the house, Mary?"

"Our Brian will be wanting to stay in it. I know he will. Christ! He can even take in boarders and send me money. He's a good lad, he is."

* * * * *

On the night of November 8th, a few days before Miss Shaw, Gerald and I, and Ruth and Mary Ambrose were to leave England, an event occurred in Paris that would have historic repercussions.

A seventeen-year-old Jewish boy, despondent over the tragic fate of his parents, shot a German diplomat. It sparked events that would go down in history as "Kristallnacht." The German diplomat died on November 9th and, as a result, horrific bedlam broke out in Europe. Orders were sent out from Nazi Germany to take vengeance against all Jews. Synagogues were destroyed in retaliation, shop windows were shattered, and thousands of books were burned in mass bonfires. Worst of all, thousands of innocent Jews were arrested, tortured, and shipped off to death camps. It was the beginning of Adolph Hitler's Nazi policy, known as the "Final Solution to the Jewish Problem."

* * * * *

"I going have to ask the good angels to take care of all of you," Clarissa said, hugging Gerald to her. "'Cause when Agustus tell me 'bout all the tragedy happening around us, I wonder if God too busy these days. Now, Gerald, you is a good son and always was. You brother and sister going miss you, so will Agustus, but we will come to visit when the war over. Don't forget to write us. Somebody can send telegram if anything bad happen. And, Gerald, you already know that I love you from the bottom of my heart, so I just want to say that I have come to love Ruth, too."

* * * * *

On the morning of our departure, we met at Mile End Road because of its proximity to the shipyards. All of us were excited and heavy-hearted as we stood in the kitchen for the last time.

"I guess you know I'll be coming with you, Fiona," Jules said calmly, looking up over the top of his teacup. "It's not going to be that easy for you to get rid of me, you know. You'd have to beat me off with a stick."

Miss Shaw broke into a wide smile. I had never seen her look as surprised or as radiant. She lifted David and handed him over to Jules.

"Darling," she said, "you'll have to beat me off with a stick too. You've made me very happy. I couldn't be more pleased that you've decided to come, but here, hold our son." She leaned over toward Jules and handed him the child, much to Jules's delight.

"Come to Daddy." David wrapped his arms around Jules's neck lovingly.

I felt sad as I watched them, for I couldn't help feeling lonely despite being surrounded by friends.

"God Almighty!" Mary Ambrose cried out, startling me. She was inspecting the many pieces of luggage crowded in the hall. "Whose grip is this? It's so bloody heavy!"

"It's ours—mine and Charlie's," Elizabeth said softly. "We're coming too."

We must have all looked incredulous. Elizabeth and Charlie put down their cups of cocoa and smiled.

"We wanted to surprise you, both Mary Ambrose and I. And when the Command Pay Office released Brandon's army savings to me, it was all we needed for the journey home. So like it or not, your Captain Isra has already made the arrangements."

I was oblivious of the others in the room and took Elizabeth in my arms. I could feel her shivering, though her breath was warm, and she was as light as the air. Her salty tears brushed against my cheek, and I let her stand on top of my shoes as we waltzed exuberantly around the small kitchen. Sometimes it was her face I saw there laughing up into mine, and sometimes I saw the laughing face of Madam Hung Chin.

*****

In 1940, while we were relatively safe in Jamaica, a rain of bombs fell upon London, destroying many of London's neighbourhoods, including Limehouse. The destruction was devastating; many lives were lost, and many homes were destroyed. Mr. Brown, in an attempt to save the twins during an air raid, went back inside the house to retrieve his family before bombs hit. Because of his heroic efforts, the twins and Clarissa were spared, though he lost both his legs in the blast and would be confined to a wheelchair for the rest of his life.

*****

Ruth and Jules set up a thriving law practice in Kingston on Duke Street, not far from where I once lived with the Meitners. And Miss Shaw, who is now Mrs. Maxwell, has joined the faculty of a school she herself pioneered. It is a school for storytellers and artists. Elizabeth works alongside her, creating ceramic pieces and teaching others her craft. With a staff of six, they were able to offer courses in painting, drawing, sculpture, and print making. The school was welcomed into the community with the registration of seventy full-time students.

Gerald's services as an accountant and economist were also in demand. In spite of the war, businesses flourished in Kingston, and they relied heavily on his knowledge of international marketing. Also, two national political parties were recently formed, one of which was offered Gerald's services. It was a party headed by a Jamaican who had won the unanimous affection and staunch respect of his followers, and who also had originally come from humble beginnings before rising to become a leader. His name was Mr. Alexander Bustamante.

Mary Ambrose was in awe of the scenic beauty of the island and said she would like to stay there for the rest of her life. She was thrilled to accept a position as caregiver to the children of several foreign diplomats. "God Almighty! Now I'se going to have to always be on me best behaviour, won't I now? But who's to say that one day I won't run off with one of them diplomats? Just you watch me now, luv."

*****

Elizabeth and I were married at Holy Trinity Cathedral, where my mother had been given food. We have found contentment in each other, and I am in the process of setting up a newspaper company, specializing in world affairs, to rival the existing newspaper company. "Rivalry is good for business," Gerald had said, "and all you need are other journalists as good as yourself."

217

I have already seen for myself that there are many eager young men here in Jamaica who require nothing more than an opportunity to prove themselves, and I, for one, am more than willing to wager their success.

I have also managed, on visiting lawyers in Kingston, to reclaim the property on Luke Lane where my beloved Madam Hung Chin's shop once stood. I plan, as soon as the war is over, to build facilities to accommodate a school of dance for Jamaican children where Madam Hung Chin once taught me how to waltz.